MIND-BLOWING TRUTHS: DEMOLISHING THE STRONGHOLDS IN YOUR MIND

Adessa Holden

MIND-BLOWING TRUTHS: DEMOLISHING THE STRONGHOLDS IN YOUR MIND:

Copyright © 2025 4ONE MINISTRIES, INC

All rights reserved. No portion of this book may be reproduced, stored in a retrieval system, or transmitted in any form or by any means—electronic, mechanical, photocopy, recording, scanning, or other—except for brief quotations in reviews or articles, without the prior written permission of the author.

Published by 4One Ministries, Inc. Visit www.adessaholden.com for more information on bulk discounts and special promotions, or e-mail your questions to info@4oneministries.org.

The ESV® Bible (The Holy Bible, English Standard Version®). ESV® Text Edition: 2016. Copyright © 2001 by Crossway, a publishing ministry of Good News Publishers. The ESV® text has been reproduced in cooperation with and by permission of Good News Publishers. Unauthorized reproduction of this publication is prohibited. All rights reserved.

The Holy Bible, New International Version®, NIV®. Copyright ©1973, 1978, 1984, 2011 by Biblica, Inc.™ Used by permission of Zondervan. All rights reserved worldwide. www.zondervan.com The "NIV" and "New International Version" are trademarks registered in the United States Patent and Trademark Office by Biblica, Inc.™

Scripture quotations marked KJV are taken from the King James Version®. King James Version. Dallas, TX: Brown Books Publishing, 2004. Used by permission. All rights reserved.

Scripture quotations marked (NLT) are taken from the Holy Bible, New Living Translation, copyright © 1996, 2004, 2007 by Tyndale House Foundation. Used by permission of Tyndale House Publishers, Inc., Carol Stream, Illinois 60188. All Scripture taken from the New Century Version®. Copyright © 2005 by Thomas Nelson. Used by permission. All rights reserved.

Scripture quotations from THE MESSAGE. Copyright © by Eugene H. Peterson 1993, 1994, 1995, 1996, 2000, 2001, 2002. Used by permission of NavPress. All rights reserved. Represented by Tyndale House Publishers, Inc.

Scripture taken from the New King James Version®. Copyright © 1982 by Thomas Nelson. Used by permission. All rights reserved.

Design: James J. Holden

Subject Headings:
1. Christian life 2. Women's Ministry 3. Spiritual Growth

ISBN 978-1-965809-03-7

Printed in the United States of America

WHAT PEOPLE ARE SAYING ABOUT MIND BLOWING TRUTH: TEARING DOWN THE STRONGHOLDS IN YOUR MIND:

"I think Adessa is on to something here. Learning how to identify, attack and remove strongholds in our minds is critical in our quest for enjoying the freedom that Christ died for us to have. If you have been living subject to one of these strongholds in your mind, this book will equip you with the tools you need to step into new seasons of freedom in your life. Adessa's perspectives will also help you explore how to better partner with the Holy Spirit to lead you into this freedom. Get your copy today!"

-**Scott Kramer**, *Lead Pastor, GT Church, West Lawn, PA*

"Adessa Holden has created a valuable resource for people to utilize to identify and break free from strongholds that have held them back for possibly their entire lives. ***Mind Blowing Truth*** is a book that leaders can use to take individuals or groups through the process of exposing lies and revealing truth that sets them free. The illustrations in the book are so relatable, and I believe any Christian would greatly benefit from reading and applying the content to their lives."

-**Dr. Deanna Doss Shrodes**, *Author and Speaker*

"I believe wholeheartedly in the message of this book. ***Mind-Blowing Truth: Demolishing The Strongholds In Your Mind*** speaks directly to the heart of every believer's walk with God. The truths in these pages are not just theoretical ideas but practical tools that every Christian needs to embrace if they are serious about spiritual growth and freedom. Strongholds, as addressed here, are not just mental barriers but spiritual obstacles that hinder us from living in the fullness of Christ.

This book is a powerful guide, grounded in Scripture, that equips us to partner with the Holy Spirit to tear down these strongholds and walk in true freedom. I encourage you to not only read, but to deeply engage with its content. It is essential reading for every believer who desires to grow, mature, and be all that God has called them to be."

-**Pastor Shane Wilson**, *Lead Pastor, Christian Life Assembly, Camp Hill, PA*

"In her new book release, ***Mind-Blowing Truth: Demolishing The Strongholds In Your Mind,*** Adessa challenges us to put on our warrior's wardrobe to deal with the strongholds in our minds. With the help of the Holy Spirit we can face and deal with those thoughts and attitudes that defeat us. Freedom is ours!

I highly recommend this book as a manual to finding a new mindset in Christ!"

-**Laverne Weber**, *Victory's Journey Ministries*

DEDICATION

I want to dedicate this book to a few people who helped me through the process of tearing down strongholds in my life:

First, to my brother Jamie. Thank you so much for listening, listening, listening, listening, listening, listening, and then listening some more. I appreciate you so much!

Then to Laverne Weber and Sue Willis. Without you, I do not know how I would have gotten through this process. Thank you for your counsel, your advice, and even your honest correction. I hope to follow in your footsteps and help as many people find healing and freedom as you have over the years. I love you both so much!

TABLE OF CONTENTS

1	Why Does It Bother You So Much	9
2	The Root Of The Problem	25
3	Unconfessed Sin	41
4	Overcoming The Pain Of Your Past	61
5	That's Not What I Learned Growing Up!	77
6	The Truth About False Teaching	97
7	Where Do We Go From Here?	115
8	Taking Your Thoughts Captive	133
	Note From The Author	151
	Video QR	155
	Bibliography	157

Chapter One
"Why Does This Bother You So Much?"

I hope I never forget the night the Holy Spirit asked me this question. It had been a difficult day. Leading into this night, my brother and I had been earnestly praying and asking God for wisdom. We were actually experiencing a wonderful problem—the ministry we lead together was growing. In fact, it was growing so much we were having a difficult time keeping up. Knowing that continued growth would necessitate change, we'd spent months asking God to show us what lifestyle and work changes we should make to keep up with His plan for our lives and the ministry.

As we prayed, the Holy Spirit was faithful. After much prayer and discussion with my brother, I made a decision. I truly believed that it was the right decision and that the Holy Spirit was leading me in that direction. Jamie agreed, and we moved forward.

Then came the resistance. In a very cruel way, my decision came under attack. *"Why would you EVER want to do THAT?"*

My character was attacked. I was told every possible thing that could go wrong and filled with fears of looming devastation in the future. Finally, I was told that neither my Mom (who is in Heaven) nor God would like this decision.

That night, I went to bed defeated. All I wanted was to feel God's loving presence comfort me and say, *"Poor 'Dessa. You didn't deserve that."* I wanted pity and comfort and to be reassured that I was the victim.

That is not what happened. Instead, while I wanted to wallow and whimper, God wanted me to put on my warrior's wardrobe.

I can still remember as clear as day how, after I'd cried for a while, the Holy Spirit reminded me of 2 Corinthians 10:3-6:

> *For though we walk in the flesh, we are not waging war according to the flesh.*
>
> *For the weapons of our warfare are not of the flesh but have divine power to destroy strongholds.*
>
> *We destroy arguments and every lofty opinion raised against the knowledge of God, and take every thought captive to obey Christ, being ready to punish every disobedience, when your obedience is complete. (ESV)*

What? This wasn't what I was expecting. What did this mean? That's when the Holy Spirit spoke to me as clearly as if He were in the room and said, *"Why did this bother you so much?"*

"Uh, excuse me? Didn't you see what happened back there?"

"Yes, but why did it bother you so much?

Is it possible that the real problem isn't the person you think you're fighting but that their words triggered your fears and strongholds in your mind? If you didn't already kind of agree with what they were saying, wouldn't you brush it off and go on?

Isn't the real issue that needs to be addressed inside of you?"

Mind. Blown.

Because it was true, the real problem was that I had issues inside of my own heart and mind, hurts from my past, my fears, and my questions as to whether or not this new direction was God's will.

It started about six months before this very bad day. Through a series of events, the Holy Spirit showed me that if I wanted to continue to grow into who God wanted me to be and fulfill His plan for my life, I had to deal with the lingering effects of some false teachings about gender roles and family that my parents learned and adopted into our family when I was still a very young girl. For months, I'd been working on identifying, removing, and replacing these man-made legalistic ideas with God's Word.

Honestly, I thought I was experiencing another round of inner healing—working through the heartache and trauma of the past so that God could bring healing and restoration. But that night, the Holy Spirit showed me that while an element of inner healing was involved, I was tearing down strongholds in my mind. Looking again at 2 Corinthians 10:3-6 and then at Ephesians 6:12, I realized that the real battle I needed to fight wasn't against another person but inside of my mind.

> ***For we are not fighting against flesh-and-blood enemies, but against evil rulers and authorities of the unseen world, against mighty powers in this dark world, and against evil spirits in the heavenly places. (NLT)***

The Holy Spirit's final words that night were, *"This isn't a time to cower. It's a time to stand firm and fight, not against people, but against the strongholds in your mind."*

This concept was mind-blowing for me. It was the first time I'd really seen my struggles as *"strongholds."* Yet, like a spotlight providing clear illumination and direction, realizing I was tearing down strongholds gave me a clear path and fresh motivation to continue moving forward with God's plan.

The next day, I began researching and studying to determine "What is a stronghold?"

I started with Joyce Meyer's book, *"The Battlefield of the Mind."* In this book, she defines a stronghold as *"an area in which we are held in bondage (in prison) due to a certain way of thinking."*[1]

A stronghold is "an area in which we are held in bondage (in prison) due to a certain way of thinking." Strongholds are usually hidden and protected.

Interesting. I definitely felt like *"a certain way of thinking"* was keeping me in bondage.

The next thing I learned as I studied was that, by definition, strongholds are protected areas.

"In the Old Testament, the word 'stronghold' usually referred to a literal physical place—a cave or a mountain—that was difficult to detect or assault. It was a fortified dwelling used as a means of protection from an enemy."[2]

Strongholds aren't out in the open saying, *"Hey, look over here, I'm what's causing you heartache."*

They are hidden. Usually, we hide them because we can't bring ourselves to face the truth.

Sometimes, it's because the truth will hurt too much. Other times, it's because we'd have to face the truth about people we love and admire and have put on a pedestal. We've made their word unquestionable rather than recognizing they are just human beings with their own problems.

Sometimes, it's because it's all we've ever known, and we're afraid to step out of our comfort zone. You may enjoy the problem and don't want to give it up.

Whatever the reason, we mentally and emotionally protect and coddle this area so that it can never be identified as the root of the problem.

Yet, it isn't until we allow the Holy Spirit to enter those protected areas that we can genuinely experience true freedom.

"It was with this imagery in mind that Paul adapted the word 'stronghold' to define powerful, vigorously protected spiritual realities. In 2 Corinthians 10:3-6, Paul uses the word 'stronghold' to describe a source of defense for the devil, where demonic or sinful activity is actually defended within us by our sympathetic thoughts toward evil."[2]

"Okay, wait a minute, hold the phone. Does having a stronghold in your life mean that you are demon-possessed?"

Absolutely not.

It's important to remember that Paul spoke to the Christian church in Corinth in these verses. As the Fire Bible says: *"God's Word teaches that because God's Holy Spirit lives within each true follower of Christ, a Christian cannot be demon-possessed. God's Spirit and demons can never live in the same body. (2 Cor 5:15-16). Demons may, however, influence the thoughts, emotions, and actions of Christians who fail to follow and respond to the leading of the Holy Spirit. (Matt 16:23, 2 Cor 11:3, 14)".*[3]

Here's an example to help us understand what this means.

I love to watch home renovation shows. One of my favorites is about people who buy old, dilapidated fixer-uppers on prime beachfront properties. Here's how the show usually goes: a couple looks at two or three houses with absolutely incredible views.

Eventually, they choose one and take possession of it.

They are the new owners, and the property belongs to them.

The old owners don't live there anymore—they give up all legal rights of possession to the property. However, that doesn't mean their influence isn't still felt throughout the house.

What do I mean? Remember I said this was a renovation show?

So even though the new owners have the legal right to possession of the property, until they renovate the house, there is usually quite a bit of *"influence"* from the previous owners.

Some of this influence is downright funky. There may be hideous color choices or some of the weirdest wallpaper imaginable. One house made a window so the people in the living room could see into the bathroom. As the new owners walk through the house, there usually comes a point where they say, *"What were they thinking?"*

Of course, most houses need more work than just a fresh coat of paint. Most of the time, the new owners must rip out walls, floors, or windows. Behind the surface, they see water damage, mold, termites, bugs, and rot. I watched one show where they found dead animals rotting in the walls of a lake house. EWWWWW!!!!!

The point is that even though the new owners have possession of the house—it fully belongs to them, and the old owner has lost all of their rights—the new owners can't fully enjoy the house or make it into the magnificent vacation home it could be until they tear out all of the problems left behind by the old owners.

The same is true with believers.

When we accept Jesus as our Savior, He takes possession of our lives. We belong to Him, and the Holy Spirit lives inside of us. We no longer belong to Satan, and we cannot be demon-possessed.

> ***For he has rescued us from the kingdom of darkness and transferred us into the Kingdom of his dear Son, who purchased our freedom and forgave our sins. -Colossians 1:13-14 (NLT)***

However, just because we are now under Christ's Lordship doesn't mean we are immediately and magically changed into Christ's image. No, this happens over time as we allow the Holy Spirit to work in our lives, taking one area at a time, removing our old ways of living and thinking, and replacing them with God's ways.

Mind-Blowing Truths

When we accept Jesus as our Savior, He takes possession of our lives. We belong to Him, and the Holy Spirit lives inside of us. We no longer belong to Satan, and we cannot be demon-possessed.

The technical term for these two processes is *"Sanctification."*

Sanctification is *"the process by which God is cleansing our world and its people. His ultimate goal is that everything—animate and inanimate—will be cleansed from any taint of sin or uncleanness."*[4]

Sanctification is cleansing and removing sinful patterns, behaviors, and ways of thinking from our lives.

Sanctification has two parts. The first comes salvation when Christ forgives our sins and declares us righteous before God. This type of righteousness is called *"imputed righteousness."* It means that when we accept Christ's offer of salvation, He gives us His righteousness and declares us righteous before God.

This is God's part, step one. However, it is only the beginning of the sanctification process.

The next part of sanctification is our responsibility. This involves the choice of the Christian to *"put off"* sins and *"put on"* God's ways.

> *Since you have heard about Jesus and have learned the truth that comes from him, throw off your old sinful nature and your former way of life, which is corrupted by lust and deception.*
>
> *Instead, let the Spirit renew your thoughts and attitudes. Put on your new nature, created to be like God— truly righteous and holy. -Ephesians 4:21-24 (NLT)*

Sanctification is cleansing and removing sinful patterns, behaviors, and ways of thinking from our lives.
It has two parts. The first comes at salvation when Christ forgives our sins and declares us righteous before God. The second continues throughout our lives as a Christian "puts off" sins and "puts on" God's ways.

It's like changing your clothing. You choose to *"take off"* the sins in your life—how you lived before salvation—and decide to walk in God's holy ways. This is an ongoing process in the life of a believer. It never ends. A healthy, maturing Christian will always be in the process of becoming more like Jesus. It's a sign of growth. You are healthy and growing as long as you're fighting for freedom and allowing the Holy Spirit to work on your heart.

Part of the sanctification process is allowing the Holy Spirit to show you the strongholds or the areas in your life that need to be remodeled because they are still heavily influenced by your old patterns of living and thinking and then working with Him to remove them.

"Why Does This Bother You So Much?"

How do you do this? How do you get rid of a stronghold?

Here's another home renovation story that will help us find the answer.

A few months ago, my friend purchased a new house. When she and her husband went to the bank, signed the papers, and got the keys, they became the home's new owners. The house completely belonged to them. The old owners relinquished all their property rights. They couldn't live there anymore. They couldn't even visit without my friend's permission. The house was fully and entirely under my friend's control.

Unfortunately, even though the house completely belonged to my friend, there were still remnants of the old homeowner hanging around. She and her husband had to work to make the home their own.

Right off the bat, there were some obvious things. The old owners left some of their old things lying around for my friend to clean up and throw away. It's not ideal, but it's also not a huge deal.

As time went on, more significant issues popped up. The old owners neglected the furnace and didn't repair the roof. As the new owners, my friends had to make these repairs.

Then, there was the carpet in the office. When winter came, and the heat went on, all my friend could smell was cat urine on the carpet. Now, the cat was gone. It didn't live there anymore, but its smell had a *"strong hold"* on the carpet.

This *"strong hold"* remained until my friend went through the work and expense of ripping out the old carpet and padding, cleaning up any hidden damage, and installing new flooring.

It's the same way with spiritual strongholds in our lives.

Even though Christians belong completely to Jesus and are filled with the Holy Spirit, we still have to partner with the Holy Spirit and do the work of tearing down the strongholds in our hearts and minds.

How do we do this?

First, you have to identify the stronghold.

> Even though Christians belong completely to Jesus and are filled with the Holy Spirit, we still have to partner with the Holy Spirit and do the work of tearing down the strongholds in our hearts and minds.

Then, you need to find the source of the stronghold.

Finally, you have to tear it down. It must be demolished.

Here's the truth about strongholds—they aren't just going to roll over and die.

They are going to put up a fight.

They won't just wilt away and dissolve on their own. No, you will have to do the work to rip them out of your life.

If you want to experience absolute freedom, you'll need to give the Holy Spirit permission to show you every truth, heal every pain, and clean out every area you previously protected.

In the words of HGTV, this is not a remodel—it's a gut job.

If you've ever lived through a home remodeling project, you know how messy and difficult demolition can be.

Yet, it is the only way to get to the root of the problem, clean up the mess, and bring about complete restoration.

No, it's not picture-perfect... it's messy.

There's heartache, pain, and even some anger. There may even be push-back from friends or family who do not want to change.

"Why Does This Bother You So Much?"

So why not just let the stronghold stay?

Because as long as we allow strongholds to remain in our lives, we cannot become the people God wants us to be or do the things He wants us to do. We can't experience the freedom and abundant life God has for us. We remain prisoners of our past.

This is not what I want. I want to grow and become everything God wants me to be. I genuinely want to be free of guilt, fear, and any lies. I want to live in truth, even if it isn't pretty. I want to walk in God's freedom rather than fear.

Even if this means some hard days as I fight the battle to tear down strongholds, the victory is worth the fight.

This is the decision I made the night the Holy Spirit asked me, *"Why does this bother you so much?"*

As soon as I discovered that there were strongholds in my own mind causing me pain, I said, *"Let's do what it takes to tear them down."*

The same can be true in your life. Freedom is available to all who will open the door to the Holy Spirit and say, *"Come renovate my life. As You point out strongholds that need to be removed, I will work with You to tear them down."*

That's why I'm inviting you to take this journey with me.

Along the way, I'll share what I've learned about tearing down strongholds and the tools the Holy Spirit has given us to win the spiritual battle of the mind.

Together, I know we can do more than just dream of what we can be someday.

We can learn to fight to gain our freedom.

Are you ready to get started?

Group Study Questions ...

1. Read each section of 2 Corinthians 10:3-6 and write down how you can practically apply it to your life.

   "For though we walk in the flesh, we are not waging war according to the flesh."

   "For the weapons of our warfare are not of the flesh but have divine power to destroy strongholds."

   "We destroy arguments and every lofty opinion raised against the knowledge of God, and take every thought captive to obey Christ, being ready to punish every disobedience, when your obedience is complete."

2. Did you ever think you were fighting with a person or a situation when you were really fighting a stronghold in your mind?

"Why Does This Bother You So Much?"

3. What is a stronghold?

4. What does it mean when we say a stronghold is a protected area?

5. Why can't a Christian be demon-possessed?

6. What are the two parts of sanctification? How do they have different roles in the life of a Christian?

7. Read Ephesians 4:21-24. How do we *"put on our new nature?"*

8. What are the three parts of tearing down the strongholds in our lives?

9. What does the story of my friend's new house teach us about removing strongholds from our lives?

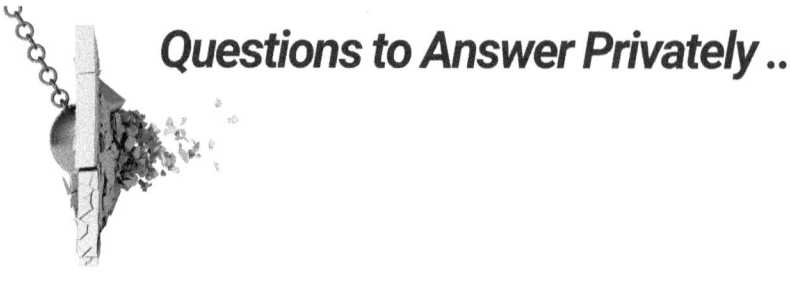

Questions to Answer Privately ...

1. While reading this chapter, did the Holy Spirit point out any strongholds in your life?

2. Are there any *"protected areas in your life"* where the Holy Spirit is not allowed to enter or disturb?

3. Are you willing to do the work to demolish any strongholds in your life?

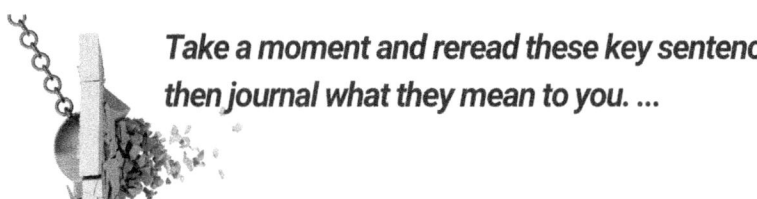

Take a moment and reread these key sentences, then journal what they mean to you. ...

1. Strongholds aren't out in the open, saying, *"Hey, look over here. I'm what's causing you heartache."* They are hidden. We usually hide them because we can't bring ourselves to face the truth.

2. A healthy, maturing Christian will always be in the process of becoming more like Jesus. It's a sign of growth. As long as you're fighting for freedom and allowing the Holy Spirit to work on your heart, you are healthy and growing.

3.   Here's the truth about strongholds—they aren't just going to roll over and die. They are going to put up a fight. They won't just wilt away and dissolve on their own. No, you will have to do the work to rip them out of your life.

Chapter Two
The Root Of The Problem

It was a bright, warm, sunny day in early Spring. After a long, hard winter, I couldn't wait to open the doors and windows and fill my house with fresh air. It was glorious!

That is until I noticed the bugs. They looked like tiny little flies all over one side of my living room. I was horrified.

Quickly, I shut the door and started cleaning up the mess. I moved the furniture and vacuumed everything in sight, assuming the tiny creatures appeared because I hadn't cleaned well enough. Yet, nothing seemed to be dirty.

When we realized the pests were coming from outside the house, I called an exterminator. For years, we'd been spraying bug repellent around the foundation of our home, but apparently, it wasn't working. It was time to bring in the professionals.

I was entirely unprepared for what they had to say.

I couldn't believe my ears when the exterminator delivered the awful news that my *"fly-like"* pests were actually TERMITES.

In the next twenty-four hours, we discovered that the destructive little devils had been invading my house for a while. Thankfully, we caught them before they damaged the foundation. (Seriously, I'm so thankful.) However, we still had to pay the exterminators to kill all the bugs and set up a maintenance system around my house. We also had to fix the front door where the little pests were having a feast. So frustrating!

One of the things the exterminators try to do while they are *"exterminating"* is to get to the source of the problem. My problem came from an old stump in my front yard.

Unfortunately, I know the stump well. I was there when they cut down the tree. I was also there when my parents decided to save money and not have the tree stump removed. Instead, we covered it with decorative rocks and planted pretty bushes around it.

For years, that little garden has looked beautiful in our front yard. Yet, the whole time, the stump was rotting and attracting termites, which eventually attacked the house.

Let me tell you, getting rid of termites costs a lot more than digging out a stump! Even though it looked like we'd solved the problem by burying it, we created a larger one.

As we went through this predicament, I thought about how this situation resembles our spiritual lives. Often in life, we begin to experience difficulties. Much like I responded to the tiny bugs flying and crawling on the floor behind my sofa, our first instinct is to try to solve the problem that we can see. Still, despite our best *"clean-up"* efforts, the issue never completely disappears. Instead, it resurfaces from time to time or appears in other forms.

The Root Of The Problem

Did I forget to tell you that this wasn't the first time the nasty little bugs had ruined a beautiful Spring day? The truth was that it had been a problem for years. Like clockwork, I'd come to expect that on the first warm days of Spring or during a spike in temperatures in the Fall, the front of my house would be attacked by swarming little creatures. (The termite man called them *"swarmers."* Pretty accurate.) We tried homemade concoctions for years, throwing boiling water on the bugs and constantly vacuuming to solve the problem. Yet, year after year, they returned.

The difference this year was that I reached my breaking point and decided to do something about the issue.

Here's the fantastic part: since the exterminator identified the source of the problem and did what was necessary to solve it, the bugs have yet to reappear. It's been several years. Recently, when a landscaper removed some plants from the front of my house, he said there were absolutely no signs of termites. Getting to the root of the problem solved the issue.

The same is true when it comes to tearing down strongholds in our lives: we need to get to the root of the problem to remove it completely.

How do we do this?

The first thing that we need to do is allow the Holy Spirit to show us the root of the problem.

How do we do this?

For me, it often begins with prayer. I know there is a problem, but I can't quite pinpoint it.

"Why is this bothering me?"

"Why am I so annoyed all the time?"

MIND-BLOWING TRUTHS: DEMOLISHING THE STRONGHOLDS IN YOUR MIND

"Why do I feel angry?"

"Why did that word, that scene in that television show, that line in that song make my heart hurt so much?"

After I've eliminated all the natural reasons (hunger, tiredness, hormones, etc), I ask the Holy Spirit to show me the root of the problem so we can work together to overcome it.

> An essential element in tearing down strongholds in our lives is getting to the root of the problem so we can remove it completely.

Often, I find that the Holy Spirit is the One Who allowed the circumstances and situations causing me discomfort so that I would want to get to the root of the problem. The truth is that we are often comfortable with our issues. We're used to them. They are normal to us. We've learned how to *"work around them."*

It's like my kitchen light. I knew it needed to be replaced for years, but I didn't want to buy a new one, so I ignored the problem until it started blinking on and off every time I tried to use it. Once I couldn't avoid the strobe light show when I was cooking, I addressed the problem.

In the same way, the Holy Spirit will allow circumstances that cause us to ask, *"What is the problem, and how do I fix it?"* When our hearts are in the proper place, He is free to show us the root cause of the strongholds in our lives.

So, where exactly do strongholds come from?

Most strongholds are the result of one of four things:

- Unconfessed sin in your life.

The Root Of The Problem

- Our Experiences—Unresolved issues from your past—either things you've done or things that were done to you and how they make us view the world.

- The World We Were Born Into-Our Parents

- False Teaching[1]

Strongholds can come from any of these four or be a combination of these things. Either way, the same truth applies: you must identify the root of the problem to eradicate it from your life.

It reminds me of something my brother went through. It started in late August and early September. Almost out of the blue, he had incredible pain. Then, a white spot began to form on his big toe…almost like a blister.

At first, the doctor thought it was a stress fracture. As it worsened, they thought he was fighting an infection and put him on antibiotics. Nothing helped.

> **Mind-Blowing Truths**
>
> Most strongholds are the result of one of four things:
>
> 1. Unconfessed sin
>
> 2. Our Experiences—Unresolved issues from your past—either things you've done or things that were done to you
>
> 3. The World We Were Born Into—Our Parents
>
> 4. False Teaching

Even though Jamie lives with the daily pain of his disability, he said the tumor on his toe was the most painful thing he's ever experienced. Finally, unable to bear the pain any longer, he went to a foot specialist who said, *"There's a fluid-filled cyst in the toe."*

The only solution was to face the problem and undergo surgery to remove the cyst/tumor. Right there in the office, he had emergency surgery.

Here's the thing: even though he had to stay off his foot for the next few weeks so that the wound would heal correctly, the intense pain in his toe went away when the tumor was removed.

The same is often true in our lives. We walk around each day in pain, struggling with issues and attitudes, totally unaware of the source of the problem.

Then the Holy Spirit, by God's grace and love, says, *"The root of the problem is here. You must face the issue, tear down the stronghold, and overcome it."*

Do we always want to go through the process?

No.

Is it for our good?

Absolutely.

> **Mind-Blowing Truths**
>
> Just like the only way to get rid of the bugs was to address the issue of the stump, and just like the pain in my brother's toe could only go away by removing the cyst, so getting to the root of the stronghold in our lives is the only way to gain freedom.

The same is true with getting to the root causes of the strongholds in our lives. It isn't always pretty. Most of the time, it's painful. We are forced to remember things we'd rather forget or face the truth about people or circumstances we'd prefer to leave hidden.

And yet, the fact remains that just like the only way to get rid of the bugs was to address the issue of the stump, and just like the pain in my brother's toe could only go away by removing the cyst, so getting to the root of the stronghold in our lives is the only way to gain freedom.

While it is momentarily painful, the results last a lifetime.

The Root Of The Problem

Remember these things as you go through the process of tearing down your strongholds:

It's important to understand that the power of the Holy Spirit is essential when it comes to tearing down strongholds because it is very, very hard to identify these root causes, realize they are problematic, and remove them from our lives on our own.

Because we've lived with them, we're comfortable with them. They make up our culture and family life. We tend to accept these mindsets rather than do the work to extract them.

We hear it every time someone says, *"Everyone in my ethnicity has anger issues"* or *"All the women in my family have anxiety."*

It's what Paul is talking about when he refers to the ***"weight that slows us down, especially the sin that so easily trips us up." -Hebrews 12:1 (NLT)***

Yet, in this same verse, Paul doesn't leave any room for saying, *"Oh well, that's just the way it is."*

No, he says:

> *Therefore, since we are surrounded by such a huge crowd of witnesses to the life of faith, let us strip off every weight that slows us down, especially the sin that so easily trips us up. And let us run with endurance the race God has set before us. -Hebrews 12:1-2 (NLT)*

I love the way the Message translates these verses:

> *Do you see what this means—all these pioneers who blazed the way, all these veterans cheering us on?*
>
> *It means we'd better get on with it.*
>
> *Strip down, start running—and never quit!*

> *No extra spiritual fat, no parasitic sins. Keep your eyes on Jesus, who both began and finished this race we're in.*
>
> *Study how he did it.*
>
> *Because he never lost sight of where he was headed—that exhilarating finish in and with God—he could put up with anything along the way: Cross, shame, whatever. And now he's there, in the place of honor, right alongside God.*
>
> *When you find yourselves flagging in your faith, go over that story again, item by item, that long litany of hostility he plowed through. That will shoot adrenaline into your souls! -Hebrews 12:1-3 (MSG)*

Then it gives us a few things to remember:

> *In this all-out match against sin, others have suffered far worse than you, to say nothing of what Jesus went through—all that bloodshed!*
>
> *So don't feel sorry for yourselves. Or have you forgotten how good parents treat children, and that God regards you as his children?*
>
> *My dear child, don't shrug off God's discipline, but don't be crushed by it either. It's the child he loves that he disciplines; the child he embraces, he also corrects. -Hebrews 12:4-6 (MSG)*

Here's why we do it:

> *God is educating you; that's why you must never drop out. He's treating you as dear children.*
>
> *This trouble you're in isn't punishment; it's training, the normal experience of children… But God is doing what is best for us, training us to live God's holy best. At the time,*

discipline isn't much fun. It always feels like it's going against the grain.

Later, of course, it pays off big-time, for it's the well-trained who find themselves mature in their relationship with God. -Hebrews 2:7, 10-11 (MSG)

Then, it ends with more encouragement:

So don't sit around on your hands!

No more dragging your feet! Clear the path for long-distance runners so no one will trip and fall, so no one will step in a hole and sprain an ankle.

Help each other out. And run for it! -Hebrews 12:12-13 (MSG)

Can't you almost hear the Rocky fight music playing in the background? These verses are inspiring, telling us, *"Don't quit. Don't be discouraged. Recognize that God wants to remove strongholds from your life and change your mindset for your good! He wants you to grow! He wants you to mature! This is how you become more like Jesus!"*

So don't cower. Don't fall back! Get in the game and do whatever is necessary to remove the deep, strong roots holding you in captivity.

Will it be easy? No

Tearing down a stronghold is not for the faint-hearted. It requires strength, courage, and determination.

As a child of God, you are not called to be weak. You are destined to be a warrior—using the spiritual weapons God has given you (Ephesians 6) to tear down strongholds and align your thoughts with Christ. (2 Corinthians 10:3-6)

If I can do it, so can you. You can tear down the strongholds in your life from the root. Through the power of the Holy Spirit, you are strong enough and have the tools you need. The question is: are you ready to get started?

The Root Of The Problem

Group Study Questions ...

1. What does the story of the termites teach about tearing down strongholds in our lives?

2. What are the four root causes of most strongholds?

3. How can a stronghold in our lives be compared to a physical injury?

4. Why is the Holy Spirit's power essential in tearing down strongholds?

5. Take another look at these passages in Hebrews 12 and discuss how each section applies to tearing down strongholds in your life.

   -Hebrews 12:1-3

   -Hebrews 12:4-6

   -Hebrews 12:10-11

   -Hebrews 12:12-13

Questions to Answer Privately ...

1. Are there areas of your life where you know an issue exists but have avoided facing the truth? List these areas.

2. Why are you ignoring these problems? Be honest and specific with yourself.

3. After reading the four roots of strongholds, which are the root of the issues in your life? Do you have more than one?

Take a moment and reread these key sentences, then journal what they mean to you. ...

1. The Holy Spirit will allow circumstances that cause us to ask, *"What is the problem, and how do I fix it?"* When our hearts are in the proper place, He is free to show us the root cause of the strongholds in our lives.

2. Strongholds can come from any of these things, or they can be a combination of these things. Either way, the same truth applies: you have to identify the root of the problem so that you eradicate it from your life.

3. The power of the Holy Spirit is essential when it comes to tearing down strongholds because it is very, very hard to identify these root causes, realize they are problematic, and remove them from our lives on our own. Because we've lived with them, we're comfortable with them. They make up our culture and family life. We tend to accept these mindsets rather than do the work to extract them.

4. As a child of God, you are not called to be weak. You are destined to be a warrior—using the spiritual weapons God has given you (Ephesians 6) to tear down strongholds and align your thoughts with Christ. (2 Corinthians 10:3-6)

Chapter Three
Unconfessed Sin

In this chapter, we'll look at the first root cause of strongholds in our lives: Unconfessed Sin.

If you're like me and have a sensitive conscience, the phrase *"unconfessed sin"* can send you into a tailspin. Suddenly, you're mentally scrolling through the past few days or weeks of your life, trying to remember if there were any times when you said, thought, or did something wrong and forgot to ask God to forgive you.

Before you spiral down that rabbit hole, let me put your mind at ease. When we talk about the unconfessed sin that can form a stronghold, it doesn't refer to sin we don't know about (ways we sin subconsciously). It isn't talking about occasional accidents, mistakes, or sins.

It doesn't refer to the day you weren't feeling well and you snapped at your family or the time you accidentally swore when you dropped a brick on your foot. We're not talking about accidentally seeing an inappropriate scene in a movie while you were changing the channel and having a momentary inappropriate thought or even forgetting to confess something to God in your time of prayer.

These things things are not defiant. They are a part of being a human being. While it's important that we keep short accounts with God and confess every sin the Holy Spirit brings to our minds, we can't beat ourselves up for every minor infraction. These things happen; you ask God to forgive you and move on.

Instead, when we say that unconfessed sin can form a stronghold in our lives, we're talking about the sins that we struggle with over and over again and can't overcome or the sins that we choose to allow in our lives even though we know they are against God's Word.

> **Mind-Blowing Truths**
>
> When we say that unconfessed sin can form a stronghold in our lives, we're talking about the sins that we struggle with over and over again and can't overcome or the sins that we choose to allow in our lives even though we know they are against God's Word.
> When we live in open rebellion to God and God's Word, sin can form a stronghold in our lives because we invite it.

When we live in open rebellion to God and God's Word, sin can form a stronghold in our lives because we are inviting it in. We're basically saying, *"Come in and set up shop in my life because I have decided that this sin is more important to me than obeying God."*

Of course, most people don't actually say that part out loud, but their attitudes and choices show what's really in their hearts.

One Biblical example of this is found in Joshua 7, in which we read the story of Achan. It's important to understand that Joshua 7 occurs just days after one of God's greatest miracles and Israel's most powerful victories in Jericho. Many of you will remember the story of the Israelites walking around the walls of Jericho every day for six days, and then on the seventh day, God miraculously caused the walls of Jericho to crumble, giving Israel the distinct advantage to conquer their enemies.

Unconfessed Sin

God also gave them very clear instructions:

> ***Do not take any of the things set apart for destruction, or you yourselves will be completely destroyed, and you will bring trouble on the camp of Israel. Everything made from silver, gold, bronze, or iron is sacred to the Lord and must be brought into his treasury. -Joshua 6:18-19 (NLT)***

Simple enough..when you plunder the land, everything belongs to God. However, as we see in Joshua 7, Achan did not obey this command. Instead, he took a robe from Babylon, 200 silver coins, and a bar of gold weighing more than a pound and hid it in his tent. (Joshua 7:21)

As far as Achan could see, no one was the wiser. Only God knew, and He was not pleased.

As we see at the beginning of Joshua 7, God could not continue blessing His people with victories until the sin was removed from their camp. Rather than having a mighty victory as they did in Jericho, the Israelites were defeated—big time—when they attacked the much smaller town of Ai.

Joshua and the Israelites were shocked. What happened?? What in the world was God doing? But when they prayed, they got a response they weren't expecting.

> ***But the Lord said to Joshua, "Get up! Why are you lying on your face like this? Israel has sinned and broken my covenant! They have stolen some of the things that I commanded must be set apart for me. And they have not only stolen them but have lied about it and hidden the things among their own belongings. That is why the Israelites are running from their enemies in defeat. For now Israel itself has been set apart for destruction. I will not remain with you any longer unless you destroy the***

> *things among you that were set apart for destruction."*
> *-Joshua 7:10-12 (NLT)*

Israel has a problem—someone in the camp sinned, but they don't know who or how. Notice that even though Israel has suffered a massive defeat and thirty-six men died, Achan still didn't confess his sin.

He didn't confess after God spoke to Joshua.

He didn't even confess when the Holy Spirit began putting a spotlight first on his tribe, then on his clan, then his extended family, then his immediate family, then finally on him. It wasn't until Joshua said, *"Dude, you're the guy, repent!"* That Achan said, *"I did it."* (Joshua 7:16-21) Let's be honest: confessing after you are caught isn't repentant; it's just getting caught.

Achan was very committed to not confessing his sin!

As we examine his story, we can see several elements that are common to the unconfessed sins that cause strongholds in our lives.

1. Achan knew what God wanted and chose not to obey.

Achan didn't accidentally sin. It wasn't subconscious or a mistake. Achan knew what God said, but he chose to do the opposite.

He was disobedient and defiant.

These are two trademarks of unconfessed sins that cause strongholds in our lives. Whenever we know what the Bible says and choose to do the opposite, we are saying that our sin is more important to us than obeying God. Our choice to protect and defend our sin allows a stronghold to form and remain.

2. Achan tried to hide his sin.

This is another tell-tale sign that unconfessed sin has a stronghold in your life—you have to hide it.

Here's something I've seen throughout my life—unconfessed sin thrives on darkness and secrets. It's like fertilizer to a plant. The more you have to keep your sin quiet, the deeper the roots of the stronghold will go until it completely controls your life.

So if you have to hide it—you have a problem.

3. Even when Achan was called on the carpet, there was no sense of genuine repentance.

Even as we read Achan's confession after he was caught, we don't sense real remorse. He didn't ask his countrymen to forgive him for bringing them defeat, apologize to the families who lost their loved ones, or ask his own family for forgiveness for what he did to them. He doesn't appear repentant; he just got caught.

> **Mind-Blowing Truths**
>
> Four trademarks of unconfessed sins that cause strongholds in our lives are:
> 1. We know what the Bible says and choose to do the opposite.
> 2. We have to hide our sins.
> 3. We are unrepentant.
> 4. We excuse our sins.

Again, this is a common attitude of someone with unconfessed sin that leads to a stronghold. They aren't repentant. They don't find it necessary to confess their sin to God. They aren't sorry for how their sin hurts others. They may be sorry they got caught and have to suffer consequences, but they would have done the same thing if they had the choice to make again. Here's one last element that is common in the unconfessed sin that causes strongholds:

4. You excuse your sin.

Granted, this is not found in the Biblical account of Achan. Still, it's so common that we have to talk about it.

It's one of the biggest traps that allows people to condone their unconfessed sin rather than overcome it. We hear it all the time:

"But I can't help it; it's how I was raised."

"All the people in my ethnicity have this issue."

"God understands; He sees what I've been through and knows I NEED this."

"I have special circumstances; God's rules don't apply to me."

Yet, the problem with excusing and defending our unconfessed sin is that it is destroying us all the while. It's damaging our relationship with God, hurting our conscience, setting up a stronghold in our lives, and saying, *"From here on, I'm in control. I'll be calling the shots."*

Here's the worst part—your unconfessed sin works for your enemy, and it is trying to destroy you.

While we may think we are fooling people, God, or even ourselves, the enemy of our souls knows that we have no intention of evicting this sin from our lives. This attitude in our lives allows a stronghold to form.

So how do we prevent this or tear down a stronghold from unconfessed sin if it is already there?

1. We must be open and respond to the Holy Spirit's conviction.

One of the Holy Spirit's primary functions in the life of a believer is to convict us of our sins.

Unconfessed Sin

> *And when he comes, he will convict the world of its sin, and of God's righteousness, and of the coming judgment.*
> *-John 16:8 (NLT)*

The Holy Spirit convicts us as we hear God's Word, either as we read the Bible or listen to someone teach Biblical truth. Often, the Holy Spirit uses that truth to illuminate a sin in our lives and show us our need to repent and change.

Other times, the Holy Spirit will bring something to our memory when praying or in a time of worship. As we remember, we will feel a sense of conviction that shows us that we need to repent of a sin.

When this happens, it's like the Holy Spirit is standing in the house that is our lives, saying, *"This mess doesn't belong in God's holy house. We need to eliminate it and not allow it here again."*

When we respond to the Holy Spirit's conviction, repent, and do all we can to eliminate sin from our lives, He will strengthen us and enable us to overcome that sin.

However, we all have to admit that there are times when we don't agree with the Holy Spirit and instead try to ignore Him. Perhaps we like the sin or believe we can't survive without it. Somehow, we've convinced ourselves that *"It's not that big of a deal"* or *"I need this in my life."* We may have fallen for the lie that we cannot overcome.

When this happens, sin can form a stronghold in our lives because we are protecting it.

But when we agree with the Holy Spirit's conviction, stop making excuses and admit we have a problem. We are on the road to overcoming our sin and tearing down any strongholds that the sin has formed in our lives.

One way we do this is to **recognize we need to see our sin as God sees it and hates it as much as He does.**

One of the biggest lies in today's world is that too many people believe the lie that *"Because God loves me, He thinks I'm adorable. When I sin, He thinks it's cute. He knows it's wrong, but because of His love, He understands. He knows what I'm going through or what I've been through, and He gets it."*

Feeding into this lie, churches today don't talk about *"sin."* Instead, they talk about people's *"messes," "issues," "mistakes,"* and *"problems."*

This makes it sound nicer, cuter, less dangerous, and less serious than it actually is. It's easier for people to hear. It's less offensive.

There's only one gigantic problem: In God's eyes, sin is offensive.

Because God is holy, He is pure and complete in character. He is totally without sin and right in everything He thinks and does. God's holiness means that He is separated from all evil. Sin literally offends Him.

If we are going to be honest with ourselves and other people, we need to take sin seriously, too. Because not only is sin a serious offense in God's eyes, but it also carries serious consequences.

The Bible says, **"The wages of sin is death."** (Romans 6:23, NLT)

This doesn't just mean the physical death that entered the world when Adam and Eve sinned, but the eternal death of life apart from God in Hell for all eternity.

The fact is that sin separates you from God.

Sin can keep you out of Heaven.

And sin will reap painful consequences here on earth.

"But Des', what about grace? What about mercy? What about forgiveness and God's love???"

Unconfessed Sin

All of these things are absolutely true! They are all part of God's character and are available to everyone.

Without God's love, grace, and forgiveness, we would all be doomed to a life of destruction and eternity in Hell.

However, God's love, grace, and forgiveness are to remove our sins and give us a new life, not condone a sinful, unrepentant, rebellious life.

> **Mind-Blowing Truths**
> God sent His Son into the world to forgive sins and help us overcome them. While He is merciful and gracious in forgiving sin, that doesn't mean He condones it. Believing anything else is a big lie that only hurts the people who hear and believe it.

God sent His Son into the world to forgive sins and help us overcome them. While He is merciful and gracious in forgiving sin, that doesn't mean He condones it. Believing anything else is a big lie that only hurts the people who hear and believe it.

That's why you must stop excusing your sin, hiding it, playing around with it, and acting like it's no big deal.

You must realize that sin is serious; if it has taken up residence in your life, it must go.

3. You must confess your sin.

Once we hate our sin and are disgusted by it, once we realize that it hurts our relationship with God, others, and ourselves, we must confess our sins.

When *"we confess our sins to him, he is faithful and just to forgive us our sins and to cleanse us from all wickedness."* (1 John 1:9, NLT)

You must admit, *"Yes, this is a big problem in my life. I recognize it. I agree with the Holy Spirit that this should not be a part of my life."*

Then, you repent and ask God to forgive you.

In Psalm 51, King David sets an excellent example of how to repent when we have sinned against God.

It's interesting that even as a man who loved God, David fell into many of the same traps as Achan.

He knew God's Laws regarding adultery and murder, but still, he did it. Then, he tried to hide his sin, hoping no one would find out.

However, the big difference between Achan and David is that when David was confronted with his sin because the Holy Spirit told the prophet, Nathan, David immediately repented.

He recognized that his sin was a big deal.

He didn't make excuses, but he wholeheartedly and thoroughly repented.

Psalm 51 is the exact words that David prayed after he faced his sin. In this psalm, we see some of the attitudes necessary to thoroughly repent of our sins and demolish any strongholds they may have in our lives.

First, David thoroughly confessed his sin.

> *Have mercy on me, O God, because of your unfailing love.*
>
> *Because of your great compassion, blot out the stain of my sins. Wash me clean from my guilt. Purify me from my sin.*
>
> *For I recognize my rebellion; it haunts me day and night.*

> *Against you, and you alone, have I sinned; I have done what is evil in your sight.*
>
> *You will be proved right in what you say, and your judgment against me is just.*
>
> *For I was born a sinner—yes, from the moment my mother conceived me.*
>
> *But you desire honesty from the womb, teaching me wisdom even there. -Psalm 51:1-6 (NLT)*

Next, David asked God to forgive him and cleanse him of all unrighteousness.

> *Purify me from my sins, and I will be clean; wash me, and I will be whiter than snow.*
>
> *Oh, give me back my joy again; you have broken me—now let me rejoice.*
>
> *Don't keep looking at my sins. Remove the stain of my guilt.*
>
> *Create in me a clean heart, O God. Renew a loyal spirit within me.*
>
> *Do not banish me from your presence, and don't take your Holy Spirit from me. -Psalm 51:7-11 (NLT)*

Finally, David desires to stop sinning and live by God's ways.

> *Restore to me the joy of your salvation, and make me willing to obey you.*
>
> *Then I will teach your ways to rebels, and they will return to you.*

MIND-BLOWING TRUTHS: DEMOLISHING THE STRONGHOLDS IN YOUR MIND

Forgive me for shedding blood, O God who saves; then I will joyfully sing of your forgiveness.

Unseal my lips, O Lord, that my mouth may praise you. -Psalm 51:12-15 (NLT)

This is such an essential part of repentance and tearing down the stronghold of unconfessed sin: you do everything possible to get that sin out of your life and live differently.

> **Mind-Blowing Truths**
> An essential part of repentance and tearing down the stronghold of unconfessed sin: you do everything possible to get that sin out of your life and live differently.

You take a sledgehammer to it and destroy it. You demolish it. Whatever is necessary—whatever you must do—you do your part to get the sin and any stronghold it has formed out of your life.

This may involve:

- Confessing the sin to someone else.
- Finding an accountability partner.
- Finding a counselor for help or support.
- Making massive lifestyle changes.

Or a combination of these things.

Still, true repentance means that you will do whatever it takes to eliminate this sin from your life.

Here's the amazing part: when you decide to do everything you can to remove sin from your life, the Holy

> **Mind-Blowing Truths**
> When you decide to do everything you can to remove sin from your life, the Holy Spirit, Who lives inside you, partners with you to give you the strength to do everything you can't do on your own.

Unconfessed Sin

Spirit, Who lives inside you, partners with you to give you the strength to do everything you can't do on your own.

When your continued determination partners with the power of the Holy Spirit, together you can overcome any sin and tear down any stronghold from unconfessed sin in your life.

I love that David expresses this hope at the end of Psalm 51 when he says,

> *You do not desire a sacrifice, or I would offer one. You do not want a burnt offering.*
>
> *The sacrifice you desire is a broken spirit. You will not reject a broken and repentant heart, O God. -Psalm 51:16-17 (NLT)*

This is the hope for everyone struggling with unconfessed sin in their lives—God wants to help them overcome their sins, tear down any strongholds that have formed, and walk in freedom and victory. Because He is gracious, merciful, and loving, He wants to forgive you and change your life. He doesn't want your sin to destroy you like Achan's sin destroyed him. He wants you to have a story like David's, filled with repentance, forgiveness, change, and victory.

Today, the choice lies with you.

Are you ready to stop excusing sin, protecting it, standing guard against the Holy Spirit, and saying, *"You can't touch this?"*

Will you recognize the damage sin is causing in your lives, repent, and partner with the Holy Spirit to do everything necessary to demolish it?

This is the only path to tearing down strongholds from unconfessed sins. Repentance and demolition are your road to freedom.

Group Study Questions ...

1. What is the difference between sin we forgot or neglected to confess and *"unconfessed sin"* that forms a stronghold?

2. How does Achan demonstrate someone with unconfessed sin in their lives?

3. What are the four common elements in unconfessed sin that form a stronghold?

Unconfessed Sin

4. What role do *"defiance"* and *"disobedience"* play in unconfessed sin forming a stronghold?

5. Read Numbers 32:23 and 1 John 1:9. What do these verses tell us about getting caught versus confessing our sins?

6. List the steps to tearing down a stronghold of unconfessed sin.

7. How does the Holy Spirit work in the life of a believer to convict them of sin?

8. What does it mean to *"hate your sin as much as God does?"*

9. How were David and Achan similar? How were David and Achan different?

10. What does Psalm 51 teach us about repentance?

11. Are there any areas you would like the group to join with you in prayer?

Questions to Answer Privately ...

1. As you read this chapter, did the Holy Spirit convict you of unconfessed sin in your life?

2. Are there areas where you know God's will, but are living in disobedience?

3. Are you hiding secret sin? Are there any areas in your life you'd be ashamed to put on social media or talk about in church-areas you don't want people to see?

4. Are there sins in your life that you are excusing rather than confessing and trying to overcome?

5. What is your plan to follow David's example and thoroughly repent for your unconfessed sin?

6. Do you need to:

   -Confess the sin to someone else?

   -Find an accountability partner?

   -Find a counselor for help or support?

   -Make massive lifestyle changes?

   What is your plan to follow through with these actions?

7. Are you ready to stop excusing sin, protecting it, standing guard against the Holy Spirit, and saying, *"You can't touch this?"*

8. Will you recognize the damage sin is causing in your lives, repent, and partner with the Holy Spirit to do everything necessary to demolish it?

Unconfessed Sin

Take a moment and reread these key sentences, then journal what they mean to you. ...

1. When we live in open rebellion to God and God's Word, sin can form a stronghold in our lives because we invite it in. We say, *"Come in and set up shop in my life because I have decided that this sin is more important to me than obeying God."*

2. Whenever we know what the Bible says and choose to do the opposite, we are saying that our sin is more important to us than obeying God. Our choice to protect and defend our sin allows a stronghold to form and remain.

3. Unconfessed sin thrives on darkness and secrets. It's like fertilizer to a plant. The more you have to keep your sin quiet, the deeper the roots of the stronghold will go until it completely controls your life.

4. Your unconfessed sin works for your enemy, and it is trying to destroy you.

5. When you determine that you will do everything you can to remove sin from your life, the Holy Spirit, Who lives inside you, partners with you to give you the strength to do everything you can't do on your own.

When your continued determination partners with the power of the Holy Spirit, together you can overcome any sin and tear down any stronghold from unconfessed sin in your life.

Chapter Four
Overcoming The Pain Of Your Past

It was late at night, and Jamie and I decided to watch something funny before bed. So we turned on an episode of *M.A.S.H.* Who knew the Holy Spirit would use this episode to help me tear down a stronghold in my life?

The episode we watched centered around Hawkeye Pierce—the chief surgeon at the 4077. Almost out of the blue, he started having sneezing fits. The other doctors ran tests but couldn't find anything physically wrong with him. As time went on, his symptoms kept getting worse, but no one would figure out why.

Then they called in the army psychologist. Turns out that Hawkeye's symptoms were the result of a repressed memory from when he was a little boy. When a patient came in smelling like a swamp, it triggered his memory of almost drowning as a child. His symptoms finally went away when he remembered the trauma, worked through the anger and fear, and admitted that he hated the cousin who tried to hurt him.[1]

As I watched that show late one night, the Holy Spirit used this story to show me that there were repressed memories that I wasn't dealing with in my life. If I wanted to experience freedom and healing, I had to let Him show me things from my past that I didn't want to remember. It wasn't until I agreed with Him and unlocked the box of repressed memories that I was able to gain healing and freedom.

I remembered this story as I was preparing to write about the second way that strongholds take root in our lives: ***Through unresolved issues in our past.***

While there have been times when I have had to deal with the strongholds of unconfessed sin in my life (this is a part of every Christian's life), most of the strongholds in my life have come from unresolved issues from my past.

This can include things that you have done or that were done to you, as well as your experiences and the effects those experiences have had on your life.

Our experiences affect us for better or for worse. They influence how we view God, ourselves, and those around us. They alter our belief systems and influence our thinking.

Apart from the work of the Holy Spirit in our lives, we are the product of our experiences. We carry those experiences, the things that happened to us, and the words that were spoken to us and about us in our hearts and minds as if we were carrying a backpack.

Some of our experiences in life were very good. However, we can all agree that we've all experienced things in our lives that were traumatic and that caused us pain.

Overcoming The Pain Of Your Past

Often, because we don't want to deal with the pain or we can't deal with the pain because of immaturity or circumstances at the time, we push the pain to the back of our minds and forget about it, hoping that it will go away.

You could say we bury it or cover it up. Another term is that we *"repress it."* The problem is that unaddressed, unhealed pain in our hearts doesn't go away on its own. It just hides and creates a stronghold in our lives. Here's how my friend, Laverne Weber, describes it in her book, *"Victory's Journey"*:

"Everybody carries some junk in their backpack that they really don't need. Whether big or small, that junk weighs us down and keeps us from being all that God wants us to be.

In dealing with the healing of past pain, we need to identify past pain.

The past is anything before today. It can be from your childhood or from later in your life.

Pain is something that has caused you to suffer. That suffering cripples you and prevents you from being all that God intended you to be....

Different people react differently to pain. That can be a way of coping. God gives us the ability to shut down areas of emotion and memory when we are not able to deal with the distress. There may be whole blocks of time that seem to be missing in a person's life. The person knows something is wrong but may not be sure what it is. Other people know what happened but have shut down any emotional response. After a while, they find they have difficulty even feeling good feelings. Some people wear "masks". At first, this helps to cope with the hurt, but in time, these masks become walls to hide behind.

Often, hurting people just don't know how to come out into freedom.

Others ignore the pains of the past...

Pain that is not dealt with will find another way out, and it will often hurt someone else. It is so much better to go back prayerfully and be healed.

One of the first steps in the healing process is to identify the pain."[2]

She goes on to describe the five types of pain:

1. *Physical - severe illness or injury to yourself or a loved one*

2. *Spiritual*

3. *Emotional – hurtful relationships and rejection*

4. *Negligence – abandonment, lack of proper care and provision*

5. *Sexual (may be subtle or suggestive) – any violation of privacy in the sexual area*[3]

When left unaddressed, all of these types of pain can create powerful and painful strongholds in life. This means that our past experiences influence how we think, react, feel, and make decisions.

So, how do we overcome the pain and trauma from our past experiences so that we can think, react, and make choices through God's eyes rather than the eyes of our pain?

Once again, we must allow the Holy Spirit to show us His truth.

I have been through this process several times throughout my life. In my twenties, the Holy Spirit did a deep work of inner healing in our whole family when He exposed my Dad's lies and abuse. The book *"Finding Healing"* tells this story in-depth. Later, in my late thirties, I went through a time of tearing down false teachings that affected how I viewed myself as a single woman. The night the Holy Spirit used an episode of *M.A.S.H.* to trigger pain from my past was during my most recent time of tearing down the strongholds that

Overcoming The Pain Of Your Past

came from pain from the past. By now, I'm pretty familiar with the pattern of how this process works.

For me, it usually starts with a *"trigger."* I'll see a television show or a movie, or perhaps I'll hear a song, and it will hit my heart in an unusually painful manner.

A book triggered this last round of inner healing and tearing down strongholds. As I read, I could identify with almost everything the author said. I could relate to her fears, her anxiety, and the lies that were in her mind, causing her guilt and confusion. Each new chapter triggered a new level of pain.

It's funny—even as I write that word *"triggered,"* I'm cringing because it's been misused today. The problem is that too many people believe that if something *"triggers"* you or causes emotional pain, then you need to do all you can to avoid the thing causing the pain.

However, this is the wrong attitude. Instead, we should see the *"trigger"* as a blessing because it shows that we have an issue in our hearts or minds that needs to be healed. Once we realize the problem is there, we can get to the root of the problem, face the pain, and allow the Holy Spirit to heal us.

Here's the truth: we weren't meant to live trapped in the pain of our past. God never intended for us to be prisoners, trapped by our memories and hiding from our *"triggers."* Instead, God's will is for us to overcome our past by experiencing complete healing and then use our victory to help others going through the

> **Mind-Blowing Truths**
>
> We weren't meant to live trapped in the pain of our past. God never intended for us to be prisoners, trapped by our memories and hiding from our "triggers." Instead, God's will is for us to overcome our past by experiencing complete healing and then use our victory to help others going through the same struggle.

same struggle. (Romans 8:37-39) This can only happen when we face that pain that's set up a stronghold in our lives.

How do we do this?

As I said, the first step is to allow the Holy Spirit to show you the source of your pain when something triggers it.

In addition to convicting us of sin, **the Holy Spirit can also lead us into truth.**

> *When the Spirit of truth comes, he will guide you into all truth.* -John 16:13 (NLT)

This includes helping us remember the things from our past that are causing pain in our hearts. This has happened to me so many times. For instance, as I was reading the book I talked about above, I was completely surprised at the emotion it was stirring up. So I prayed and asked, *"What is going on? Why is this happening?"*

Before long, the Holy Spirit began helping me remember moments from my childhood that I hadn't thought about in thirty or forty years. Sometimes, I'd remember things as I prayed; other times, the memories would resurface in dreams. Sometimes, while going about my day, I'd remember something. I often asked my brother, *"Did this really happen? Am I remembering this correctly?"* only to hear, *"Yeah, it happened. And this happened, too."*

No matter how it happened, each time I asked the Holy Spirit to help me, He brought just the right memory to the surface in the right way and at the right time. Then, He was there to comfort me through the next step of feeling the pain of the memory.

Because here's the thing about repressed memories—we bury them for a reason. They hurt!!

Overcoming The Pain Of Your Past

The hard truth about tearing down the stronghold of repressed memories is that you will not only remember what happened, but you will most likely feel the pain again.

For instance, there was one particular area from my childhood that has caused me pain for years. Even though it may not seem like a big deal to others, it caused so much trauma in my life that I literally had nightmares about it for decades. Then, the Holy Spirit led me to a time of facing the truth about my past that I would never face before. It was so difficult that I went into counseling with a born-again, Bible-believing, Spirit-filled counselor. As we worked together, my nightmares turned into memories as the Holy Spirit pinpointed the source of my pain.

I will never forget the night that I relived the source of the pain in a dream. It hurt so much that I woke up and ugly cried for hours. I could literally feel the heartache that seven-year-old Adessa felt as she went through the experience. Remembering this event was one of the most painful things I've gone through in my life. However, the momentary tears and heartache of actually facing the pain led to my freedom. Having faced the pain, it didn't have control over me.

As I went through the next steps of talking about the memory with my brother and trusted friends, journaling and pouring my heart out on a piece of paper about the memory, and even being in counseling, the pain of the event left my heart like the puss leaving a wound. (Gross, I know, but accurate.) Even more importantly, as time has gone on and the wound has healed, the pain no longer keeps me in its prison. Even if the anxiety tied to this event tries to resurface, I can now logically tell myself, *"It's over. It wasn't right when it happened, but it won't happen again,"* and move on.

That is what made all the temporary and momentary pain of remembering worth it—the freedom I live in now.

Of course, the process didn't end with remembering. That was like the emergency surgery my brother had on his toe—remembering removed the poison. However, there was still the recovery process.

> **Mind-Blowing Truths**
>
> It's important that we allow ourselves the time that we need to heal—not a time to wallow, but a time to rest, to sometimes cry, to heal, to spend time with Jesus, and to soak in God's Word.

It's important that we allow ourselves the time that we need to heal—not a time to wallow, but a time to rest, to sometimes cry, to heal, to spend time with Jesus, and to soak in God's Word.

Yes, I understand that it's often impossible for us to walk away from our daily responsibilities. Remember, while I was going through this process, we were still leading a ministry and traveling for Mantour Conferences. Of course, my family still expected to be fed, and the laundry still needed to be done. Life goes on.

However, when you are in a time of healing from past pain and tearing down strongholds, you need to be intentional about making life slow down a little. Yes, you still have to do what's necessary, but during this time, you will probably have to cut back on the *"unnecessary"* to make time to rest. (After all, inner healing and tearing down strongholds is hard work!)

During this time, it's important that you prioritize spending time with Jesus—not interceding for the whole world but talking to Him about what's going on inside of you. Share your heart openly and honestly. Don't be surprised if He speaks words of comfort or Scripture to you. Remember: God wants you to heal and be free. He's pulling for you and will do all He can to help as you spend time with Him.

It's also essential that as you're healing, you prioritize time in God's Word.

Why?

God's Word will help you see how to move forward. The truth is that your life will be very different as you live without the pain in your heart. God's Word can show you how to rebuild.

The truth is that trauma is a lot like a hurricane or a tornado. The storm blows in, and it's horrific to live through, but then it goes away. The problem is that even though the storm has passed, it often leaves incredible devastation behind.

> When you are tearing down strongholds that have the root of trauma in your life, it's important that you prioritize spending time with Jesus and in God's Word.

When we ignore the pain in our hearts, we are like people who choose to ignore the damage the storm did to their homes. It's like living with broken windows or a house with no roof. Rather than dealing with the water damage, they ignore it, allowing it to breed mold and pollute the air they breathe every day.

The better way is the path most storm victims choose—after the storm has passed, you clean up the mess. You fix what is broken—tear off the old shingles and remove the water-damaged drywall. Then you replace what has been damaged with new materials and rebuild.

That's what we need to do with the trauma in our lives.

Whether a storm went through your life yesterday or decades ago, the hope is that you don't need to continue living with the damage.

Through the power of the Holy Spirit, you can overcome the pain in your heart, experience healing, and rebuild your heart and mind. You don't need to continue carrying the hurt in your past around in your mental book bag any longer.

You can experience healing.

You can tear down the strongholds that pain created.

You can have a brand new start.

> **Next to salvation, the Bible, and the Holy Spirit, emotional and mental healing is one of God's greatest gifts to His children.**

Next to salvation, the Bible, and the Holy Spirit, emotional and mental healing is one of God's greatest gifts to His children.

It gives us freedom from our past and new hope for the future. It allows us to find deliverance from bondages and lies that are literally holding us captive and keeping us from experiencing the abundant life that God has for us.

It is one of the central reasons that Jesus came to earth and died on the cross for our sins.

> *Surely, He took up our pain and bore our suffering, yet we considered him punished by God, stricken by him, and afflicted.*
>
> *But he was pierced for our transgressions, he was crushed for our iniquities; the punishment that brought us peace was on him, and by his wounds we are healed.*
> *-Isaiah 53:4-5 (NIV)*

Jesus came so that we could experience healing and freedom from the pain of our past.

Today, I don't know what wounds you are facing.

I don't know the issues in your life that the Holy Spirit may ask you to address and overcome.

I do know this: There's no greater gift you can give yourself than responding to God's offer of healing.

Don't let the fear of painful memories or rocking the boat from the truth that God wants to uncover keep you in bondage.

Will there be pain?

Yes. For a little while.

Could learning the truth and tearing down strongholds cause problems?

Yes. However, it won't really cause the problems. It will just uncover existing problems and reveal ways to find solutions.

Ultimately, any pain or difficulty you go through will be worth the effort to gain freedom.

When we allow the Holy Spirit to do His work, we will find that the Great Physician can carry us through the pain, through our recovery, and bring us to a place of unimaginable healing and freedom.

Group Study Questions ...

1. What are the five types of pain?

2. How does the Holy Spirit use *"triggers"* to uncover past pain to heal us?

3. Discuss the differences between avoiding things that trigger you and using triggers as a catalyst to change and overcome.

4. How does the the Holy Spirit's role to lead us into truth help us overcome the trauma in our lives?

5. This chapter listed several tools to help us overcome the pain of trauma in our lives and tear down strongholds. List them here:

6. How is trauma like a hurricane or a tornado?

7. Isaiah 53:4-5 is one Scripture that tells us about God's healing power. Make a list of at least three more.

8. What did this chapter teach you about overcoming wounds from your past?

9. Do you want the group to pray with you in any areas regarding this week's chapter?

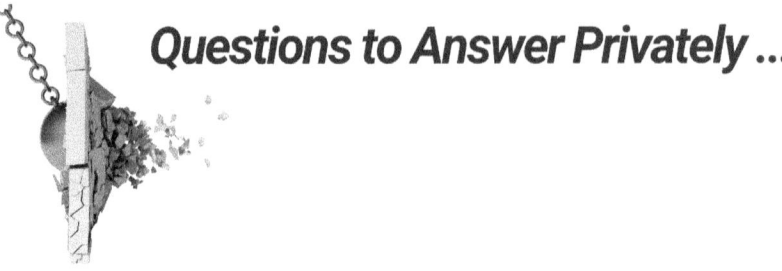

Questions to Answer Privately ...

1. As you read through this chapter, did the Holy Spirit bring any areas of trauma or repressed pain to your mind?

2. Do you know of any things that trigger you?

3. How can you use these *"triggers"* as a catalyst for healing and deliverance?

4. What steps will you take to overcome the repressed pain in your heart?

5. Will you allow the Holy Spirit to uncover past experiences in your life and tear down any strongholds they have created?

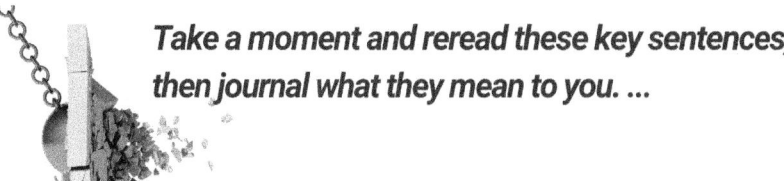

Take a moment and reread these key sentences, then journal what they mean to you. ...

1. Apart from the work of the Holy Spirit in our lives, we are the product of our experiences. We carry those experiences, the things that happened to us, and the words spoken to and about us in our hearts and minds as if we were carrying a backpack.

2. We should see the *"trigger"* as a blessing because it shows that we have an issue in our hearts or minds that needs to be healed. Once we realize the problem is there, we can get to the root of the problem, face the pain, and allow the Holy Spirit to heal us.

3. Next to salvation, the Bible, and the Holy Spirit, emotional and mental healing is one of God's greatest gifts to His children. It gives us freedom from our past and new hope for the future. It allows us to find deliverance from bondages and lies that are holding us captive and keeping us from experiencing the abundant life that God has for us.

Chapter Five
That's Not What I Learned Growing Up!

"But that wasn't how my parents did it."

I can't tell you how many times I said this phrase as the Holy Spirit was leading me through the process of tearing down strongholds in my life. I'd imagine somewhere in Heaven, Jesus must have rolled His eyes and said, *"Yes, I know. But is it possible that maybe your parents weren't right about everything, and you could try doing things God's way?"*

Of course, I'm joking. Although I am sure He must have been tired of hearing me respond this way every single time He tried to point out a stronghold that needed to be ripped down. (Even if God wasn't tired of it, I know my brother heard it more than enough!)

This was, without a doubt, the most significant root of strongholds in my life—**things we learned from the world we were born into—our parents.**

The fact is that we learn what we observe growing up.

As children, we learn our family's beliefs, prejudices, behavioral patterns, and sins. Our parents teach us everything: how to talk, how to walk, how to eat, exercise, and sleep. We learn whether or not they see education as important and pick up their attitudes about work.

They teach us about relationships. They show us how people should interact with each other in and outside of a family. We observe how they talk to each other and about each other. We see what they do in public and also see if there are changes behind closed doors.

Our parents teach us about love, marriage, and family through observation. They show us how men and women respect or disrespect each other and whether or not to tolerate abuse. Our families demonstrate to us whether or not children should be valued.

Families model how we should spend our time and our money.

Our families shape our views about government and religion.

In almost every area of life, as we grow, we watch how the people we live with function, and we believe this is normal. In most cases, we consciously or subconsciously copy the ways of our ancestors.

Even those who determine that they do not want to live the way their parents did often find themselves falling into many of the same ways of thinking and reacting as their parents did unless they allow the Holy Spirit to work in their hearts, heal their minds, and tear down any strongholds with roots tied to their parents.

This stronghold can manifest in two different ways depending on whether you had a good or bad relationship with your parents.

Those who have had a problematic relationship with their parents or even an abusive relationship can fall into one of two traps. Either they can repeat their parent's destructive behaviors and choices and excuse it, saying, *"I can't help myself. This is the way I was raised,"* or they live as constant victims of their childhood, saying, *"I can't overcome. I'll always be defeated because of what my parents did."*

Neither of these paths is God's will for His children. As we discussed in the last chapter, no one is destined to live in the pain of their past. Through the power of the Holy Spirit, you can be healed of the pain of your past and become a completely new person made in the image of Christ rather than the image of your parents.

Through the power of the Holy Spirit, you can be healed of the pain of your past and become a completely new person made in the image of Christ rather than the image of your parents.

No matter who your parents were or what they did—whether you were abused, whether your parent was an alcoholic, an inmate, or an angry person, even if your parent abandoned you—you are not destined to follow in their footsteps.

The Bible says that through Christ, you can become a new creation. Everything old in your life can be healed and overcome, and you can become new.

> ***Therefore, if anyone is in Christ, the new creation has come: The old has gone, the new is here!***
> ***-2 Corinthians 5:17 (NIV)***

But how is this possible—won't I always still be my parent's child?

No, you can choose not to follow in their footsteps. While, yes, it is natural to repeat or reflect your parents, when you become a Christian, you become a child of God.

> ***See what great love the Father has lavished on us, that we should be called children of God! And that is what we***

> *are! The reason the world does not know us is that it did not know him. -1 John 3:1 (NIV)*

As God's children, the Holy Spirit lives inside of us and is always at work in our hearts.

> *For all who are led by the Spirit of God are children of God.*
>
> *So you have not received a spirit that makes you fearful slaves. Instead, you received God's Spirit when he adopted you as his own children. Now we call him, "Abba, Father."*
>
> *For his Spirit joins with our spirit to affirm that we are God's children. And since we are his children, we are his heirs. In fact, together with Christ we are heirs of God's glory. But if we are to share his glory, we must also share his suffering. -Romans 8:14-17 (NLT)*

Look at what the Fire Bible says about verse 14:

> *"The Holy Spirit lives within a true child of God in order to lead him or her to think, speak, and act according to the principles, standards, and examples of God's Word."[1]*

> **Mind-Blowing Truths**
>
> Because you are God's adopted child and because the Holy Spirit lives inside of you, you are not destined to repeat or reflect the sins or bad choices of your parents. When you become a Christian, you become a child of God, created to reflect His image. You can choose a different path because of the changing power of salvation.

Thus, because you are God's adopted child and because the Holy Spirit lives inside of you, no person is destined to repeat or reflect the sins or bad choices of their parent. When you become a Christian, you become a child of God, created to reflect His image. You can choose a different path because of the changing power of salvation and the Holy Spirit living in your life.

That's Not What I Learned Growing Up!

But wait...there's more. (Anyone else remember those commercials?)

Not only are you not destined to repeat your parent's mistakes, but as a child of God, you are not doomed to living as a victim in the prison of what your parents did to you in the past.

As children of God, we are not called to be victims but victors. As we said in the last chapter, it is not God's will that you stay trapped in the prison of any physical, emotional, sexual, or mental abuse. You can be an overcomer through the work that Jesus did on the cross and the power of the Holy Spirit to heal you from your past experiences.

God has made a path forward for you that will heal the painful memories of your past.

By walking through the healing steps we discussed in the last chapter, you can tear down any strongholds this pain has established in your heart.

You don't have to lie down and die, convinced that you will always be the victim of your parent's choice.

You can get up, put on your warrior's clothes, and do the work necessary to overcome every bad experience you had.

You can say, *"I'm not going to be a victim anymore...I will be free."*

As you make that choice, the Holy Spirit will partner with you to give you all the help, strength, courage, and wisdom you need to become a victorious child of God.

Here is the hope for everyone who has a challenging relationship with their parents:

You don't have to follow in your parent's footsteps.

You don't have to be a victim of your parent's failure.

MIND-BLOWING TRUTHS: DEMOLISHING THE STRONGHOLDS IN YOUR MIND

As a child of God and a new creature in Christ, *"because of my parents"* doesn't have to be your prison.

> **Mind-Blowing Truths**
> You don't have to follow in your parent's footsteps. You don't have to be a victim of your parent's failure. As a child of God and a new creature in Christ, "because of my parents" doesn't have to be your prison.

You can overcome and become a new person who reflects the image of your Heavenly Father. How awesome is that!

Now to those on the other side of the coin: those with good relationships with their parents. Believe it or not, this can also cause a stronghold we need to tear down. (I know, it's mind-blowing.)

Those with good relationships with their parents tend to get caught in the stronghold of wanting to do everything just like their parents did. They have so much respect, love, and loyalty for their parents that they cling to everything their parents did and want to repeat it. Sometimes, this is good if you follow a godly example. The problem comes when you make an idol out of the person you respect, and following in their footsteps becomes more important than following God's will for your life.

Here are some clues that this may be an issue:

- You care more about what your parent thinks than what God thinks of your choices. This can be a need for approval or a fear of disapproval.

- You refuse to see that your parent is a human being with faults and struggles of their own.

- You believe everything your parent says, does, and believes is Gospel truth.

- You really struggle when the Holy Spirit leads you in a direction different from your parent's life.

- You argue with the Holy Spirit if He shows you that your parent's beliefs were not an accurate reflection of God's Word.

If you struggle with any or all of these things, you may have a stronghold in your life that needs to be addressed. I learned this lesson through experience. While *"Finding Healing"* tells the story of how I learned the lessons of breaking strongholds from a challenging relationship with a parent (my Dad), years later, the Holy Spirit started showing me some strongholds that resulted from my relationship with my Mom.

Here's the thing: I had a good relationship with my Mom. Like all relationships, there were issues; she wasn't perfect, but it was that last line I had a hard time facing for a large part of my life.

When the Holy Spirit wanted to work on areas of my heart that resulted from fears or false doctrines I learned from my Mom, it freaked me out.

Because Mom and I were very close and because I knew her passion for Jesus and her love for her family, it was very difficult for me to face the truth that there were areas in her life where she was wrong. It was hard for me to face that much of what she taught me about a woman's role in God's kingdom came from the perspective of an abused woman. Even after God did a miraculous work in our family and set us free from abuse, she was still working on overcoming the issues that came from years of being abused. Even though she didn't mean to, she passed on her fears and bad ideas she was taught to me.

This was really hard for me to face.

One of the reasons the strongholds remained in my life for so long is that I guarded them. I protected them. I was so loyal to my Mom that I wouldn't allow the Holy Spirit or anyone else to point out ways she was wrong.

I couldn't begin demolishing strongholds in my life until I took my Mom off the pedestal I put her on growing up. I had to realize she was a fallible human being who had her own struggles, her own issues from her past and was on her own journey of experiencing healing. She was living through some challenging circumstances while tearing down her own strongholds.

As I've gone through this process, I've realized that I'm not the only one struggling with this issue. Many people have parents, grandparents, teachers, pastors, and even coaches who greatly impacted their lives. They love them. They respect them, and they are so appreciative of the positive influence they've had in their lives. They knew the heart of the person they loved and that they wanted to please God and do what was right. They were just human and hadn't overcome all of their issues.

Because of their loyalty, they are blind to the weaknesses of the person they love. They view them as infallible. Their words are always true. They try to live up to the standards they set.

It's much like the Israelites felt about Abraham, Moses, and David. To the Jews living in the New Testament, these men were heroes of the faith. They looked up to them, respected them, and wanted to be just like them.

Then Jesus—the literal Son of God—comes on the scene and starts teaching about the fulfillment of God's promises to Abraham, Moses, and David.

How do the people respond?

"But Moses said..."

"But Abraham taught..."

"David wrote..."

That's Not What I Learned Growing Up!

Here's the thing: these guys were great men. They were God's men fulfilling His purposes in their time.

But they were also human beings who had some big problems in their lives! They were far from perfect.

Moses killed a man. (Exodus 2:12) Even though he was God's man leading the people out of Egypt, he still had an anger management problem. We see it when he broke the original Ten Commandments (Exodus 32:19) and when he struck the rock when God told him to speak to it. God saw this as such a problem that Moses could not enter the Promised Land because of his disobedience. (Numbers 20:1-13)

Abraham lied to get out of trouble (Genesis 12:10-20) and slept with his slave because he didn't believe God would fulfill His promise. (Genesis 16)

David committed adultery with Bathsheba, and his personal life and family were a mess. (2 Samuel 11-18)

Does this mean they weren't great men with close, personal relationships with God?

Absolutely not!

These men were the cream of the crop. Moses was so close to God that he had to wear a veil to hide God's glory, which shone off of his face after being with God. (Exodus 34:29-35) David was called *"a man after God's own heart"* (1 Samuel 13:14, Acts 13:22), and every future king of Israel and Judah was compared to him. Abraham was the father of many nations and the father of all who are justified by faith. (Romans 4, Galatians 3:29)

But they were also human beings. They were imperfect.

When we defend those we love and hold to the things they passed on to us rather than listen to the voice of the Holy Spirit, we follow the example of the Israelites who rejected Jesus to follow human heroes.

> **Mind-Blowing Truths**
>
> When we defend those we love and hold to the things they passed on to us rather than listen to the voice of the Holy Spirit, we follow the example of the Israelites who rejected Jesus to follow human heroes.

This just isn't right.

As God's children, we must follow God's ways and God's Word and fulfill God's purpose for our lives. When we can follow another's example as they are following God, that is great. However, whenever God leads us in a new direction or shows us the truth, we should never respond with, *"But that's not how my parents did it."*

We are called to follow God, not our parents.

Recently, when I started watching a new show called *"Buddy Valastro's Cake Dynasty,"* the Holy Spirit drove this point home to me. (I know, it's weird that the Holy Spirit uses television and movies to talk to me, but He does.)

I watched his first show, *Cake Boss*, many years ago on TLC. Back then, his children were babies, and the entire business occurred in a small business in Hoboken, NJ. I don't know if that show went off the air or I just got bored. Either way, it has been at least a decade since I watched it.

Now he's back with a new show, and everything is different. First, his kids (the babies and toddlers in the first) are grown and working in the bakery. The business has grown, too. They now have bakeries and restaurants all over the country. Instead of working from a basement, the main headquarters is now a factory. It's a massive change.

Still, in almost every episode, Buddy talks about doing things the same way his father taught him to do them. He means he's still using the same recipes, still dedicated to quality, and working hard just like his Dad taught him. Yet, each time, I think, *"Let's be honest, there's nothing here like your dad did things."* All of the expansion brought massive changes.

The Holy Spirit has used this example to speak to my heart as I've been watching. He showed me that just like Buddy's business couldn't grow if he'd done everything exactly like his Dad did in the small family bakery, sometimes we need to let go of the *"way we've always done things"* or *"the way someone else did things"* so that we can grow and follow God's will for our lives.

The fact is that all growth necessitates change.

Change doesn't mean you disrespect or do not appreciate those who have come before.

Neither does admitting that those who came before us had struggles they didn't overcome.

It just means that, like Buddy, *the Cake Boss*, you are taking the foundation they gave you and building on it. You're taking their seed and allowing it to grow and expand.

I've learned that I can love and respect someone and still admit, *"They were human. They had problems. Not everything I learned from them was good—some was really bad."*

I'm learning that just because my parents were godly or did extraordinary things does not mean that I am destined to live exactly as they did or even live in their shadows. Our calling is greater than simply trying to fill someone else's shoes.

My identity is not just being my parents—it comes from being a child of God.

The same is true for you: God's plan for your life may be totally different from His plan for your parent's life. He may call you to go further in life than your parents did, or He may call you to walk in a completely different direction altogether.

Whatever God's plan, we need to follow Him.

We need to build our own legacy.

So here's one last story: While I was working on this book, we were preparing for another year of Mantour Conferences. The theme was *"Unbreakable,"* and it had a boxing motif. We watched every *Rocky* and *Creed* movie to find quotes to put in the *Unbreakable Daily Bible Reading Plan* for that year. (I am now far too fluent in this genre.)

One day, while we were watching *Creed*, a scene jumped out at me.

Adonis Creed is preparing to fight when he receives a surprise gift from his mother, Mary Anne. It was a surprise because she was not thrilled that he was boxing and was giving him the silent treatment.

When the gift arrived, he opened it to find boxing shorts exactly like his father's. The only difference was that the name *"Creed"* was on the front, but Adonis' name, *"Johnson,"* was on the back.

The note that was attached said, *"Build your own legacy-Ma."* (2)

The message was clear—fight and win the battle for yourself.

If you've ever seen *Creed*, you know this was a challenge for Adonis (Donnie). Born the illegitimate son of the great boxer Apollo Creed, young Donnie had a lot going on inside him.

He wanted to live up to his father's reputation as a boxer, yet he was angry at his father for dying and leaving him alone. Most of all, as he told Rocky near the end of the fight, he needed to prove to himself and the world that he wasn't a mistake. Emotionally, the dude was a mess.

That's why the message was so important. In those few words, Mary Anne said, *"It's time to stop living in the pain and anger from the past. It's also time to stop living up to your father's greatness. It's time to build your own legacy. Fight for yourself. Be who you were meant to be."*

This needs to be the attitude of every person who wants to tear down a stronghold with roots tied to their parents.

We need to follow God and build our own legacy.

Forgive your parents for their failures.

Admit they were human beings with their own struggles and issues.

Realize that you are a child of God and allow the Holy Spirit to help you heal, help you let go of the past, and learn to live as a child of God fulfilling the plans He has for your life.

MIND-BLOWING TRUTHS: DEMOLISHING THE STRONGHOLDS IN YOUR MIND

Group Study Questions ...

1. How do our parents or the people who raised us influence our lives?

2. Read the following Scriptures and discuss how each one gives us hope that we are not destined to repeat our parent's mistakes.

   -2 Corinthians 6:17

   -1 John 3:1

   -Romans 8:14-17

3. Read these verses and discuss how they provide hope that we can experience healing and victory rather than remain victims of our parents' choices.

   • Psalm 34:18

   • Psalm 147:3

That's Not What I Learned Growing Up!

- Isaiah 61:1-4

- Luke 4:18-19

- Isaiah 49:15

- Romans 8:37-39

4. What are the signs that we have made a godly parent or mentor an idol?

5. What does the example of the Israelites telling Jesus, *"That's not how our forefathers did it,"* teach us?

6. How can we admire someone's godly character traits without ignoring their flaws and failures?

7. What does it mean to *"Build your own legacy?"*

8. What truth stood out to you most in this chapter?

9. How can the group pray for you this week?

Questions to Answer Privately ...

1. How did your parents influence your life?

2. How would you describe your relationship with your Mom?

3. How would you describe your relationship with your Dad?

4. Have you believed the lie that you can't gain victory in your life because of the way you were raised?

5. Do you feel destined to repeat your parent's mistakes or like a victim of their choices?

6. What did you learn in this chapter that will help you overcome this mindset?

7. How can you practically apply this to your life?

8. Are there any areas where you have made your parents an idol? Are you more concerned about following in their footsteps than following God's will for your life?

9. What is your plan to overcome this stronghold? What did you learn from this chapter that you can practically apply in your own life?

That's Not What I Learned Growing Up!

Take a moment and reread these key sentences, then journal what they mean to you. ...

1. Those who have had a problematic relationship with their parents or even an abusive relationship can fall into one of two traps. Either they can repeat their parent's destructive behaviors and choices and excuse it, saying, *"I can't help myself; this is the way I was raised,"* or they live as constant victims of their childhood, saying, *"I can't overcome. I'll always be defeated because of what my parents did."*

2. No person is destined to repeat or reflect their parent's sins or bad choices. When you become a Christian, you become a child of God, created to reflect His image. You can choose a different path because of the changing power of salvation and the Holy Spirit living in your life.

3. You are not doomed to living as a victim in the prison of what your parents did to you in the past. As children of God, we are not called victims, but victors.

4. When we defend those we love and hold to the things they passed on to us rather than listen to the voice of the Holy Spirit, we follow the example of the Israelites who rejected Jesus to follow human heroes.

Chapter Six
The Truth About False Teaching

One of the things that surprised me most as I studied strongholds was that they can be formed in our minds from false teaching.

It seriously blew my mind. Until then, I knew that unconfessed sin, trauma, and ideas passed onto us by our parents or the environment in which we were raised influenced our thought patterns. However, false teaching playing a role was a new concept for me.

And yet...

When I looked back on the months preceding the Holy Spirit's showing me that I needed to tear down strongholds in my thinking, it was clear that the false teachings my parents learned when I was a child played a significant role.

My story is simple. I was almost five years old when my parents came to know Jesus and began attending our local Pentecostal church.

Everything about this life was new to them, and my Mom was very eager to learn all she could about God's ways and apply them to our lives. So, when our church organized a bus trip to a conference advertised to teach the secrets of how to live in God's kingdom, my parents signed up.

Because I was only six or seven, my brother and I didn't attend the conferences. We stayed with our grandparents, who let us stay up late and eat ice cream before bed. All I remember was how excited my Mom was about everything she was learning and that my parents came home with big books reinforcing the principles they had learned. Over the next few weeks and months, many new rules and ways of doing things were introduced in our house, as Mom was excited to start obeying what she learned.

Mom was a true believer. She wanted to learn and obey as much of God's ways as possible. As a young believer, she was told that this seminar taught God's ways, and she wanted to obey God.

Another element that came into play was that my Mom grew up in a very dysfunctional family filled with abuse and alcoholism. More than anything, she wanted a normal life—a happy family. She wanted a strong marriage and for my brother and me to have a better life than she did. Because these teachings promised to deliver these things, Mom soaked them in like a sponge. She lived it, taught it, and defended it.

Looking back, I don't know what my Dad really believed, but at the time, it seemed that he, too, believed this teaching. After finding out in my twenties that so much of his life was a lie, I still don't know if he really believed the teachings they learned or if he liked that the teachings seemed to give him permission to continue the patterns of abuse and control that he learned as a child and carried into our family.

The Truth About False Teaching

You see, my Dad also grew up in a very abusive family controlled by alcohol. However, unlike my Mom, he didn't crave a fresh start. Instead, he denied that it happened and determined that no one would ever abuse him again. Instead, he became the abuser, the manipulator, and the controller.

The best thing that could have happened to my parents was if the church they attended had helped them work through their childhood traumas, overcome, and learn new behavioral patterns. Instead, excited by the eagerness and energy of new converts, they immediately put my parents to work in the church. They got positions and titles like *teacher, board member,* and *elder.* At this conference, they were also given a lot of legalistic, man-made rules to follow. Ultimately, these rules caused the existing problems to continue in our family and gain a deeper stronghold.

Here's the problem with a lot of the people who follow these teachings—they are people who genuinely want to please God. Then, along comes this man who says, *"I've studied, and this is what the Bible says and means. If you love God, you must do it."*

So they do. At great pains to themselves, they do it.

The only thing is that it's false teaching—twisted Scripture. But when it's ingrained in you and reinforced, it becomes a part of you. It's something you have to remove by force if you want to be free. You literally have to pull it down because it has such a powerful hold.

Here's the thing: most people are blind to the strongholds in their lives that come from false teaching. I know I was. Our whole family was blind to the fact that it was even false teaching until we went through our first round of finding healing and tearing down strongholds in our lives when I was in my twenties.

During this time, we learned that not only was the man who led the conferences leading a hypocritical, double life and abusing the people who worked for him, but the Holy Spirit began showing us that his teachings were twisted, manufactured rules rather than proper interpretations of the Scripture.

As we learned the truth and experienced freedom, we learned that it is not God's will for a man to have complete control over a family. We learned that God doesn't condone abuse—He hates it, and we went through years of counseling and working on our hearts to overcome the abuse in our lives.

We'd gained freedom! We saw the truth. Honestly, after discovering that these were false teachings and that the man who taught them was a false teacher, I thought this part of my life was over. I didn't think about it for twenty years.

And then...

As I said at the beginning of the book, we started asking the Holy Spirit to show us the changes we needed to make so that our ministry could continue to grow and we could fulfill God's plan for our lives.

As I said in the last chapter, each time the Holy Spirit would show us something that needed to change, whether during prayer or at another person's suggestion; my answer would be, *"That's not what I learned from my parents (particularly my Mom)."*

At the same time, I started reading a book about a woman who grew up in a similar legalistic false teaching and was surprised that I could identify with many of the author's fears, guilt, and struggles.

Then we watched a documentary that was like a bright spotlight saying, *"This was your life."*

All of these things combined were the catalysts the Holy Spirit used to reveal that even though I never went to one of the conferences, even though there were parts of the teaching that I resented growing up, and even though we knew that both the teacher and the teachings were false, there were still roots of this false teaching in my life causing me to resist the changes the Holy Spirit wanted.

Once again, I was mind-blown.

And yet…it was so true.

My next response was, *"Get it out of my head NOW!"*

Even though my attitude was correct, it's impossible for forty years of indoctrination to just vanish. Instead, it required hard work, lots of tears, and a willingness to let go of lies and embrace God's truth.

So what did I do? More importantly, what can you do if you find that you have a stronghold of false teaching in your mind?

First, you have to be willing to see the truth.

This may be hard because it's likely that you respected your teacher. Understand that the teacher doesn't necessarily have to be the man or woman who stood on a stage or wrote a book with false teachings. You may have received false teaching from a well-meaning parent, pastor, Sunday school teacher, grandparent, or other person who influenced your life. Even though they loved Jesus and wanted to live for Him, at some point, they were the victims of false teachings.

Mind-Blowing Truths

To tear down a stronghold that has it's root in false teaching you need to be willing to see the truth.

This is what happened to me. My Mom thought she was passing along the keys to the kingdom—this is how you live for God and receive His highest blessings. She meant well when she obeyed it and taught it to my brother and me, but she was misinformed. For me, the first and most difficult part of tearing down the stronghold of false teaching was admitting that my Mom was wrong.

Other people have an attachment to false teachers. They are enamored by their charm, their charisma, or the message they present. I remember when the scandals broke with Jimmy Swaggart and James Baker in the 1980's. While the mainstream media was overjoyed to see the ministry fall, some people I knew were genuinely heartbroken because they had an attachment to the ministry and the leaders. It's difficult to recognize that someone you followed, admired, and trusted was leading you down the wrong path. However, if you are following a false teacher, recognizing this will be the first step to your freedom.

The next step will take time, but it is well worth the investment.

As the Holy Spirit leads, you need to compare the individual teachings you received against Biblical truth.

How do you do this? When dealing with teachings about the Bible, it's essential to:

1. Hold up the false teachings against what the Bible says. The Bible is always true, so if their teachings differ, it is false.

2. Use reliable study tools, such as commentaries and Bible dictionaries, to gain a deeper understanding of the Scriptures.

3. Seek advice from trustworthy, knowledgeable sources to gain insights on complex biblical topics.

The point is that studying the Bible is the only way to unravel the knots of false teaching that pollute our minds.

We need to imitate the behavior of the Bereans in Acts 17:10-12. Notice that when the Jews living in Berea heard Paul, they didn't just accept what he was saying at face value. Instead, they returned to the

The Truth About False Teaching

Scriptures and checked it out. Every Christian must take up the Bereans' practice as their own.

In the present day, just as in the New Testament era, both true servants of God and false teachers claim to preach God's Word. This is not a new issue in Christianity. Throughout the New Testament, we see Jesus, Peter, Paul, and John warning believers about the dangers of false teachings and false doctrines. It is our responsibility to discern the truth.

Mind-Blowing Truths

To tear down a stronghold that has it's root in false teaching you need to compare the individual teachings you received against Biblical truth.

In Matthew 7:15, Jesus says, *"Beware of false prophets, who come to you in sheep's clothing but inwardly are ravenous wolves." (ESV)* Then, in Matthew 23, He calls out the scribes and the Pharisees as hypocritical false teachers.

In Acts 20:29-30, Paul tells the elders of the church in Ephesus that false teachers will come and why they will come:

> *I know that after my departure fierce wolves will come in among you, not sparing the flock; and from among your own selves will arise men speaking twisted things, to draw away the disciples after them. (ESV)*

Paul warns the church in Corinth that false teachers will appear to be godly people with godly intentions, and yet they are not:

> *For such men are false apostles, deceitful workmen, disguising themselves as apostles of Christ.*
>
> *And no wonder, for even Satan disguises himself as an angel of light. So it is no surprise if his servants, also, disguise themselves as servants of righteousness. Their end*

will correspond to their deeds. -2 Corinthians 11:13-15 (ESV)

The New Testament books, including Galatians, Ephesians, Colossians, Thessalonians, The Pastoral Epistles, Titus, 2 Peter, 1, 2, and 3 John, and Revelation, all address the issue of false teachings and false teachers. These false doctrines caused confusion and division in the early church, and the apostles, like Paul, Peter, and John, warned against these teachings and instructed believers on how to deal with them.

> **Mind-Blowing Truths**
> As Christians, we need to be aware that false teaching and false doctrine have always been and will always be a problem.

As Christians, we need to be aware that false teaching and false doctrine have always been and will always be a problem.

What is new today is that the digital age has given false teachers an incredible opportunity and platform to share their lies. With little investment, training, or accountability, someone calls themselves a Christian teacher and spreads their false teaching around the globe like wildfire.

It's also important to recognize that false teachings and false teachers come in all shapes, sizes, and backgrounds. And they aren't all conservative or legalistic. That's just what influenced me. Many other false teachings are just as dangerous.

For example, there is progressive Christianity, which is the exact opposite of legalism. Rather than teaching rules and regulations, it teaches that because God loves us, He wants us to be happy. So, if something makes you happy, then God approves of it.

Rather than saying that *"everything is a sin,"* they deny that sin exists. They also deny that the Bible is God's Word, that there is only one True God, and that Jesus is God's Son, Who came into the world to save people from their sins. They deny a literal Hell because a loving God would never send anyone to Hell. They even say the crucifixion didn't happen and call the idea of such a thing *"cosmic child abuse."*

Clearly, this is a false teaching; yet, because many of its proponents are charismatic, relatable, and very funny, books and videos containing this teaching are infiltrating churches and teaching false doctrine.

Another big false teaching within Christianity is the **"prosperity Gospel."**

"Just send this minister or ministry a generous gift, and they guarantee health, wealth, and a problem-free life."

They've even got Scriptures to back it up. The problem is that many of these Scriptures are misused, taken out of context or twisted. Other verses like 2 Timothy 3:12, **"Yes, and everyone who wants to live a godly life in Christ Jesus will suffer persecution" (NLT)**, are completely ignored.

Other false teachings to beware of are:

-Any teaching that raises the prophecy or teaching of a man or institution to the same level as the Bible.

This is always a red-flag warning sign. The Bible is the inspired, inerrant, and infallible Word of God (2 Timothy 3:16). Although God uses prophecy to guide His people, no prophecy is ever equal to the inspired Word of God. All teaching and prophecy should be tested and judged against God's Word for accuracy.

-Any teaching that encourages the worship of angels or saints is false teaching.

This includes Catholicism. I am not saying that a Catholic person cannot be a Christian. If a person attends a Catholic Church but accepts Jesus as their personal Savior, they are a Christian. However, the fact is that the core teachings of Catholicism, with the worship of saints and angels, are false teachings. This is the false teaching of saying that Jesus is not enough, you also need to pray to angels and saints, which Paul wrote against in Colossians 2:18-19.

> Rather than take an "oh, well, that's just how it is" attitude, we need to take the attitude of Jesus, Peter, Paul, John, and many others throughout church history and do all we can to keep our doctrine and teaching pure.

I could go on and on because there are so many false teachings and false teachers in the world. They all have the same result: twist God's Word and draw people away from God's truth.

Rather than take an *"oh, well, that's just how it is"* attitude, we need to take the attitude of Jesus, Peter, Paul, John, and many others throughout church history and do all we can to keep our doctrine and teaching pure.

Watch your life and doctrine closely. Persevere in them, because if you do, you will save both yourself and your hearers. -1 Timothy 4:16 (NIV)

We also need to help others inside and outside the church avoid falling into the trap of false teaching.

As Christians, we cannot ignore this issue.

Jesus did not, and God's Word does not. We must not simply believe every teaching that we hear. Even if the teacher is charismatic, persuasive, or funny, or even if it sounds like it should be in the Bible, we can't take a new or new-to-us teaching at face value.

Instead, we must always be on our guard against false teaching.

We must judge every teacher and every teaching against the Word of God.

The Truth About False Teaching

We need to know essential theological truth and how it should be practically applied to our lives.

We must be able to discern the difference between true Biblical teaching and false teaching, not just for our benefit but also for those who are following in our footsteps. For ourselves, we must detect and avoid false teachings so that we don't fall into sin or walk away from our true faith in Christ. Have no doubt that is the goal of the enemy—to lead you away from a personal relationship with Jesus through false teaching.

> **Mind-Blowing Truths**
>
> We must be able to discern the difference between true Biblical teaching and false teaching, not just for our benefit but also for those who are following in our footsteps.

Still, we can't be content to simply ensure our safety. We need to avoid any hint of false teaching so that we can help others—especially those who are new or immature in their faith—avoid this trap of the enemy.

Sometimes, I wonder what would have happened if the mature believers at our local church had discerned that the false teaching that deceived my parents was wrong. What if, rather than endorsing it because it was popular at the time or it catered to their particular prejudices and fears, the church leadership would have exposed it?

We will never know, and I'm not blaming anyone. Honestly, most of the people who could accept responsibility have passed away. Instead, I allow this thought to remind me of every Christian's responsibility to discern and reject false teaching so that we can accurately obey the Bible and teach others to do the same.

If we have any strongholds of false teaching in our minds, we must tear them down.

As believers, we must Biblically educate ourselves to spot false teachings and teachers, stand against them in our own lives, and help others see the truth about God and His Word.

The Truth About False Teaching

Group Study Questions ...

1. In the first chapter, we defined a stronghold as *"an area in which we are held in bondage (in prison) due to a certain way of thinking."*[1] Using this definition, how can false teaching be the root of a stronghold in our lives?

2. The first chapter discussed how strongholds are usually *"protected places."* How do we tend to protect and defend false teachings in our minds?

3. How do you discern if a belief is a false teaching or Biblical truth?

4. What are some tools you can use to help you discern Biblical truth?

5. What example did the Bereans set for us in Acts 17:10-12?

6. How do we practically follow their example?

7. Read 2 Timothy 3:16 and discuss the dangers of false teachers/teachings who give their prophecies or teachings the same authority as Scripture.

8. How did Jesus and the apostles view and address false teachings and teachers?

9. Read 1 Timothy 4:16. Why must we avoid false teachings--both for ourselves and others?

10. What steps are we practically taking to discern false teachings, avoid them, and help those who have fallen into this trap?

The Truth About False Teaching

Questions to Answer Privately ...

1. Have you ever been the victim of a false teaching or false teacher?

2. Are you protecting or defending a false teaching because you have an attachment to the person who taught it?

3. As you read this chapter, did the Holy Spirit show you any areas of false teaching you need to overcome?

4. What is your plan to learn Biblical truth on this topic?

5. Are you actively involved in Bible reading and Bible study? If not, what is your plan to make these activities a consistent part of your life?

6. What steps are you taking to follow Paul's instructions to Timothy in 1 Timothy 4:16?

7. Do you need help overcoming the influence of false teachers and teaching in your life? Are you willing to seek the help you need to tear down this stronghold in your life?

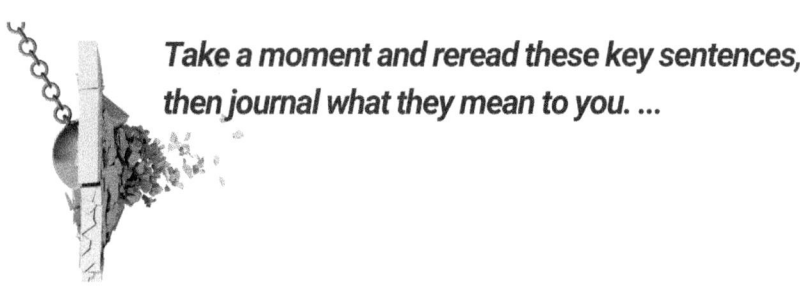

Take a moment and reread these key sentences, then journal what they mean to you. ...

1. Studying the Bible is the only way to unravel the knots of false teachings that pollute our minds.

2. As Christians, we must be aware that false teaching and doctrine have always been and will always be a problem.

3. All false teachers/teachings have the same result: twist God's Word and draw people away from God's truth.

4. We must always be on our guard against false teaching. We must judge every teacher and every teaching against the Word of God.

We need to know essential theological truth and how it should be practically applied to our lives.

5. We must discern the difference between actual Biblical teaching and false teaching, not just for our benefit but also for those following in our footsteps.

Chapter Seven
Where Do We Go From Here?

In the last few chapters, I've talked about the lessons I've learned as I've worked with the Holy Spirit to tear down the strongholds of past experiences, generational iniquities, and false teachings in my life.

But if I were reading this book, I'd say, *"Great information. Very helpful. But how do I tear down this stronghold in my own life?"*

In this chapter, we answer this question.

Step #1: Agreeing With the Holy Spirit

For me, tearing a stronghold begins with agreeing with the Holy Spirit when He points out an area that needs to be addressed. Often, this starts with me being surprised that the issue even exists until the Holy Spirit shines His light on a dark, hidden area of my mind. After that, I usually struggle to accept it.

My first response is usually, *"This can't be true."* Once I realized, *"Okay, this is my life,"* I moved on to *"But is it really that big of a deal?"*

This is often the case for many people. The Holy Spirit starts stirring things in their hearts and minds, orchestrating circumstances to heal their hearts, and their first response is denial.

Tearing a stronghold begins with agreeing with the Holy Spirit when He points out an area that needs to be addressed.

And yet, true freedom and healing cannot come until we move beyond denial and say, *"I realize this is a problem in my life, and I want to overcome it. I don't want it to control or hurt me anymore."*

When you reach a point where you say, *"I want freedom, deliverance, and healing more than I want my next breath,"* you're ready to start tearing down strongholds.

This is true no matter what your battle. Whether it be overcoming anger, abuse, sexual addiction, drinking, lying, false teaching, or any other sin or issue, Alcoholics Anonymous has it right: It all starts with overcoming denial and admitting you have a problem.

True freedom and healing cannot come until we move beyond denial and say, "I realize this is a problem in my life, and I want to overcome it. I don't want it to control or hurt me anymore."

Step #2: Prayer.

Really, it's the best place to start. After all, God already knows what's going on, so He won't be shocked. You can talk to Him about the issues you've become aware of and tell Him you want to be free.

This is also a great time to practice the spiritual discipline of repentance. When we humbly confess our sins to God, it breaks any hold that the enemy has on our lives. It's our confession that we no longer want the enemy's influence in our lives—we want to clean it all up and allow the Holy Spirit to have His way in every room of our lives.

Where Do We Go From Here?

> ***If we claim we have no sin, we are only fooling ourselves and not living in the truth. But if we confess our sins to him, he is faithful and just to forgive us our sins and to cleanse us from all wickedness. -1 John 1:8-9 (NLT)***

Confession is also the first step to emotional and mental healing.

Another important part of prayer in healing is pouring out your heart to God. As we're tearing down strongholds, we must understand that it's not a sin to do this. In fact, the Bible encourages it.

Psalm 62:8 (ESV) says, **"Trust in him at all times, O people; pour out your heart before him; God is a refuge for us."**

As we look at the great men and women of the Bible, we see them often going to God and telling Him everything they thought and felt —the good, the bad, and the downright ugly. Don't believe me? Look at the Psalms, the Book of Job, or Jeremiah. Notice that even though these words were written by some of God's most incredible, righteous men, they had some powerful thoughts and feelings they brought before God. Yet, God never turned away from them or rejected their honesty. Instead, He met them where they were and helped them overcome, heal, and grow even deeper in their relationship with Him.

Looking back on some of my conversations with God, I must admit that I'm happy He was the only one listening. I'm very sure that if I had said some of the things I said to Him to a person, they'd have condemned me as a backslidden sinner. Yet, God never did.

Maybe it's because God doesn't just know our thoughts and feelings. He also knows what caused them. He also knows WHY we think and feel the way we do, often to a greater extent than we do. That's what He can show us as we pray to Him.

"What do you do if you can't find the words?"

Step #3 Talk to God Using Your Prayer Language

When I am hurt or upset, verbal interaction is often difficult for me. Still, I know that I need to talk to God to process my feelings and get the emotions, lies, and memories out of my heart. During times like these, I will often choose to speak in tongues and allow the Holy Spirit to pray through me.

> *And the Holy Spirit helps us in our weakness. For example, we don't know what God wants us to pray for. But the Holy Spirit prays for us with groanings that cannot be expressed in words. And the Father who knows all hearts knows what the Spirit is saying, for the Spirit pleads for us believers in harmony with God's own will. -Romans 8:26-27, (NLT)*

Essentially, speaking in tongues during prayer is a declaration of surrender, a way of saying, *"I am at a loss on how to pray about this situation. Holy Spirit, I yield to Your guidance in my prayers."*

When we engage in prayer using our spiritual language and yield to the Holy Spirit's intercession, we can be confident that our prayers align with God's will. I have often experienced that as the Holy Spirit intercedes through me, it dismantles mental barriers. Soon, the Holy Spirit brings to light the things I need to confess or discuss with the Heavenly Father. It often reveals the root of the problem, a crucial step towards progress.

Step #4: Journaling

Journaling is one of the best ways to discover what is inside your heart and mind. The great thing about journaling is that you can say ANYTHING. You can write down how much you hate a person or situation, how horrible you think they are, how wrong they treated you, and how you wish bad things would happen to them while you watched (okay, that's a bit too honest).

Where Do We Go From Here?

You can say whatever. You can get out every single emotion you have and then destroy it. Burn it or shred it because you don't need it around.

Still, it's out of you and not in your heart and mind anymore.

I can't tell you how many journals I've filled with genuine feelings that I needed to release from my heart and mind, be honest with myself and God, repent of my feelings, and move on and move forward in health. As I was tearing down the stronghold of false teaching, the thoughts, feelings, and memories came so fast that I eventually grabbed my laptop and started typing so I could keep up.

Journaling works! If you need to write out your prayers to talk to God and clean out your soul, then do it. Whether you speak or write, you're communicating with God and pouring out your heart to Him.

Step #5: Talking

Another essential part of this process was talking with a trusted friend about what I was remembering, the emotions I was experiencing, and what the Holy Spirit showed me. For instance, the pain was incredible when the Holy Spirit began showing me how false teaching was affecting my views of women in ministry—specifically, walking in my own calling. And it didn't manifest as tears—no, I got angry.

I needed to figure out where to start, so I called one of my most trusted friends. She's a little older than me, and she has years of experience in counseling and inner healing. Talking to her and hearing her perspective helped me so much! Her words set me back on a path where I could journal my feelings and find freedom.

However, talking didn't stop there. After an afternoon of journaling, I spent three hours talking to my brother. I can't tell you how much it helped. (Seriously, he has been amazing through all of this. He gets extra props for listening to me throughout this process. Thank God for him!) He and other friends I talked to helped me see the truth and find freedom.

I believe that we need to get things out in the open. We need to talk about the things that bother us so that they don't always keep us bound inside.

Of course, it's essential that you talk to a Christian—but not just any Christian—someone you can trust.

We know that you can't tell everything to everyone. Some people are untrustworthy and will tell your secrets to anyone who will listen. There are also people who will use what we tell them to hurt us. Don't talk to people who have this reputation. Avoid gossips, busybodies, or people who seem to know everything about everybody.

However, you can't let bad apples ruin the whole bunch. Don't let the fear of gossip keep you from finding the genuinely godly people willing to listen and help you through your issues.

Just be wise and talk to people or several people that you know you can trust. Maybe talk to your pastor, a pastor's wife, or a godly, mature friend you can trust and open your heart up to about what's happening in your life.

At first, while going through this process, I just talked to Jamie and my friend who works in counseling. However, one of the final steps of my healing was talking to a few friends whom I really love and trust. Sharing my testimony with them helped the wounds in my heart heal. It created callouses and enabled me to recover faster and walk in freedom.

Step #6: Counseling

As the Holy Spirit worked on my heart, there were times when I could work through my issues by talking with my brother or friends in ministry. However, there came a point when the pain was so great that I found it necessary to seek help from a professional counselor. I have absolutely no regrets.

This is often a tool that God uses in our lives to help us overcome our past and tear down strongholds.

Here are a few tips for finding a counselor:

1. Make sure you go to a Bible-believing, Spirit-filled counselor.

Not all counselors are created equal. Even though most counselors are well trained and have good intentions, if you want to experience true healing and freedom, you must find a born-again, Bible-believing, preferably Holy Spirit-filled counselor.

Psalm 1:1 (NKJV) says, *"Blessed is the man who walks not in the counsel of the ungodly, nor stands in the paths of sinners, nor sits in the seat of the scornful; but his delight is in the law of the Lord, and in His law he meditates day and night."*

Because true health and freedom can only be found in the truth of God's Word, you must find a counselor who will give you advice and wisdom that comes from and agrees with the Word of God.

2. Ask the godly people in your life for recommendations.

Ask your pastor if they can recommend someone. Many churches offer counseling as part of their ministry. If your church doesn't, ask your pastor for a recommendation of a trusted church that does. A good pastor will not see this as competition, but rather understand that Christ's body works together to help people.

There are also Christian counseling centers available. Again, your pastor or the staff at your church may be able to recommend a center in your area. If you cannot find one, I recommend my friend Sue

Willis' ministry, *Beyond Survival Ministries*. They do online counseling, which may help.

3. Even if it's a Christian counseling center, read through their statement of beliefs.

Don't just go online and pick anyone. Instead, check them out.

Here's what's essential: **never fall for the lie that counseling is unnecessary or a waste of time.**

Counseling is an investment in yourself. It's always worth the time and money. A good counselor will help you see things you can't see and point you in the right direction when you don't know where to turn.

Step #7: Forgiveness

As you work through this process, there will be times when you must choose to practice forgiveness.

Yes, I know, when you are hurt and are in pain, and you are working through trauma, *"forgiveness"* can sound like a dirty word. However, it is a necessary part of the healing process.

The truth is that someone dumped garbage all over you. It wasn't your fault; they had no right to do it. However, now the choice rests with you—will you live covered in the garbage or shake off the trash, take a bath, and move on?

Mind-Blowing Truths

Almost every stronghold you tear down will involve forgiving those who hurt you.

Straight truth: Forgiveness is how you shake off the garbage.

Almost every stronghold you tear down will involve choosing to forgive those who hurt you.

Where Do We Go From Here?

Even though it isn't easy, it is crucial because unforgiveness and bitterness are often the roots of strongholds in our lives. Hebrews 12:15 warns us against allowing these roots to form.

> ***See to it that no one fails to obtain the grace of God; that no "root of bitterness" springs up and causes trouble, and by it many become defiled; (ESV)***

But what do we do if they have already formed and hold your thought patterns hostage?

We have to rip the root out by saying, *"What happened was wrong—it never should have happened—they were completely 100% wrong. But I'm not going to let their sinful choices keep me in bondage for the rest of my life. I will turn them over to God and set myself free by choosing forgiveness."* If any more roots or memories pop up, you apply forgiveness over and over and over again until the stronghold is gone.

Just in case you've received any false teachings about forgiveness, here are a few Biblical facts:

Forgiveness is not condoning the other person's behavior as acceptable or no big deal.

It isn't a get-out-of-jail-free card for people who aren't really sorry and don't want to change their lives.

When I realized that forgiveness wasn't saying, *"Oh, it's okay that you did this, or it's no big deal,"* that's when I could put things into perspective and stop blaming myself for the pain inside my heart.

Forgiveness doesn't mean you have to forget.

Realistically, you can't forget what happened. It's part of your story. Forgiveness will heal your heart and take away the pain when you remember. That's how I can write this book or tell my story in a sermon: because it doesn't hurt anymore. The memory doesn't have anger or hate attached to it anymore. I can't forget the facts, but I no longer have to live trapped in the pain.

Forgiveness doesn't mean you don't bring it up again.

Talking about issues is the key to freedom. Talking is healthy. Suppressing hurts, and keeping secrets is unhealthy. God wants us to be healthy.

Forgiveness doesn't mean you have to put your heart on the line to be hurt by someone who is unrepentant and unchanged.

Just because God commands us to forgive does not mean that He wants us to allow people to abuse us, demean us, or diminish our dignity without establishing boundaries. That would be unwise. God wants His children to be wise.

Healthy boundaries are choices that you make to proceed in a safer, healthier, and more beneficial manner to live a peaceful life.

Forgiveness is not about the other person.

Forgiveness is a gift you give yourself. It's how you choose to let the other person to God and move on with your life.

Realizing these things has helped me embrace forgiveness. I hope it will help you, too.

Okay, enough about forgiveness… what's next?

Let's talk about starting the rebuilding process. The best place to start this is:

Step #8 Searching the Bible for Answers

As I was going through the process of tearing down the stronghold of false teaching our family was taught when I was a child, one of the most shocking things to me was that much of what we were taught was God's ways weren't even in the Bible.

They were man-man, twisted distortions of Scripture or just some guy's idea that sounded good.

But I couldn't stop there. After identifying the false teachings, I had to compare them to the Bible. As I took the false teachings one by one and searched for Biblical answers, I could see that God's ways were very different from what I was taught. Knowing that God's Word is truth, I chose to follow God's ways rather than man's ways.

2 Timothy 3:16-17 says, ***"All Scripture is inspired by God and is useful to teach us what is true and to make us realize what is wrong in our lives. It corrects us when we are wrong and teaches us to do what is right. God uses it to prepare and equip his people to do every good work."*** **(NLT)**

Not only did the Scriptures help me find the truth, but they also provided me with a weapon to fight the enemy when he came back time and again, trying to get me to fall for his familiar lies.

This is another thing you should beware of: even after you do the work and use all of God's tools to tear down strongholds in your life, the enemy will still come around from time to time and attack you with familiar thoughts, hoping that he can reestablish a stronghold.

That's why it's so important that we fill our minds with God's Word--so that when these attacks come, the house of our mind has an arsenal with which to fight.

Step #9 Living in Freedom

One of the most critical steps to maintaining our freedom after we tear down a stronghold is making conscious choices to stop living in our old ways and take steps to live in freedom. I know this is challenging. Still, it was something we must do.

> *But don't just listen to God's word. You must do what it says. Otherwise, you are only fooling yourselves. For if you listen to the word and don't obey, it is like glancing at your face in a mirror. You see yourself, walk away, and forget what you look like. But if you look carefully into the perfect law that sets you free, and if you do what it says and don't forget what you heard, then God will bless you for doing it. -James 1:22-25 (NLT)*

As this Scripture says, it isn't enough to learn that you were headed in the wrong direction—you need to turn around and go the right way.

> **Mind-Blowing Truths**
> One of the most critical steps to maintaining our freedom after we tear down a stronghold is making conscious choices to stop living in our old ways and take steps to live in freedom.

When we replace the strongholds in our lives with God's Words and His way of living, we can enjoy the fruits of living under the influence of the Holy Spirit rather than our old way of life. We'll talk more about this in the next chapter.

These steps have worked for me—at least, it's a summary of them. You can read about each step more in-depth in the companion study, *"Mind-blowing Truth: Steps to Healing."*

Now, it's time for you to get started. Which step will you take first on your journey to complete freedom from strongholds in your life?

Where Do We Go From Here?

Group Study Questions ...

1. This chapter lists nine practices that will help you find healing and tear down strongholds in your life. List them here:

   1.

   2.

   3.

   4.

   5.

   6.

   7.

   8.

   9.

2. What role does confession play in emotional and mental healing?

3. How do you feel about the idea that you can say anything to God?

4. How does praying in tongues help us when we don't know how to pray?

5. Explain how journaling helps you find healing and tear down strongholds in your life.

6. Why is it essential to go to a born-again, Spirit-filled counselor?

7. This chapter listed truths about forgiveness--things it is and things it isn't. List them here, then discuss these truths.

8. Why do we need to spend time in God's Word as we go through the process of finding healing and tearing down strongholds?

9. How can you apply James 1:22-25 to what you've learned in this chapter?

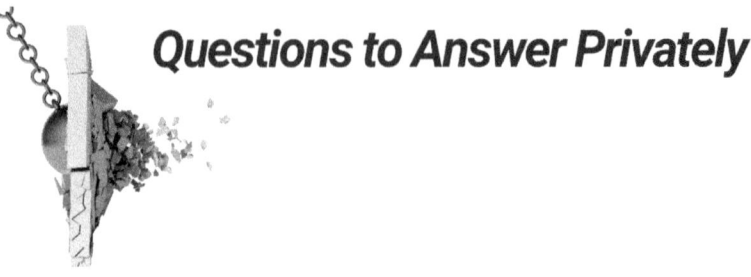

Questions to Answer Privately ...

1. As you read this chapter, did the Holy Spirit stir your heart to any particular practice and say, *"This is something you need to implement in your life?"*

2. Create a plan for HOW to start implementing these practices into your life.

3. List one to three godly, reliable, mature people you could talk about what the Holy Spirit is doing in your heart.

4. What did you learn about forgiveness in this chapter?

5. As you read, did the Holy Spirit bring someone to your mind that you need to forgive?

6. What steps will you take to start the forgiveness process?

7. How do you plan to spend time with God in prayer and His Word? When, where, and how can you schedule reading the Bible and prayer in your life?

8. How can you apply James 1:22-25 to what you've learned in this chapter?

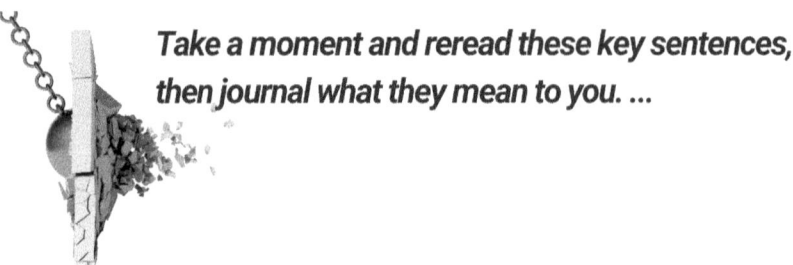 *Take a moment and reread these key sentences, then journal what they mean to you. ...*

1. True freedom and healing cannot come until we move beyond denial and say, "*I realize this is a problem in my life, and I want to overcome it. I don't want it to control or hurt me anymore.*"

2. When you reach a point where you say, "*I want freedom, deliverance, and healing more than I want my next breath,*" you're ready to start tearing down strongholds.

3. Almost every stronghold you tear down will involve forgiving those who hurt you, yourself, and others.

Chapter Eight
Taking Your Thoughts Captive

"Lorelai, stop it!"

As soon as I heard those words, I knew what my brother meant.

It started earlier in the Fall during football season. For those who don't know, I share a house with my brother and my father. Most of the year, Jamie and I watch the same television shows. However, when football season comes, we have a deal where, unless the Denver Broncos are playing, he watches football on his laptop, and I watch whatever I want on the television. When the Broncos play, he gets the TV while I use a computer. It's a grossly lopsided arrangement that benefits me, but it works for us.

Anyway, as Jamie was watching football that fall, I indulged in one of my favorite guilty pleasures—watching the *Gilmore Girls* for the umpteenth time. Only this time, as I watched I noticed something I'd never seen before. Whenever the main character, Lorelai Gilmore, was being mistreated, when people took their frustrations out on her, when they were overreacting or just being nasty, she would become adorable, charming, funny, and almost childlike to calm them down and get them to stop being mean to her.

As I watched her repeat this pattern over and over throughout the show, I realized I do the same thing. When I'm in an extremely tense situation, when people are angry with me, or when I have to tell someone something I know they aren't going to like, I become funny, agreeable, and super excited. My voice even changes and becomes more high-pitched and childlike to calm the situation and say, *"See, I'm doing what you want. I can make you like me. You can't be mad at me when I'm this funny and adorable. Don't you want to calm down and stop the yelling or mistreatment?"*

It's a survival mechanism I learned growing up in a house where there was too much tension and emotional abuse. However, watching the show, I realized, *"I don't want to do this anymore. I don't want to play this game and completely change who I am to appease someone else's moods."* Later on, my brother and I talked about it, and I told him I really wanted to change.

That's why Jamie knew he had permission to hold me accountable and remind me of my resolve when, two days before Christmas, I was falling back into old patterns.

We were in the kitchen. Jamie and I were cooking, and my Dad was in a mood—moping, pouting, and making passive-aggressive comments about my decision to order take-out for Christmas Eve rather than cook a ham. Honestly, I didn't make the decision to spite him. Jamie and I don't really like ham, and it makes me feel sick, so I decided to pick up food at a restaurant for Christmas Eve and make a special dish we all enjoyed on Christmas Day. However, as the holiday approached, my Dad's mood started bothering me. I could feel the tension, and my stomach started churning into knots.

Taking Your Thoughts Captive

Just then, my Dad noticed that I was making one of his favorite side dishes, and he realized I hadn't abandoned all Christmas traditions. That's when I kicked into my best Lorelai Gilmore impression. My voice changed, and I became ultra-perky, cute, and appeasing as I pointed out all of the food I was preparing that he liked. As I tried to cheer him up and appease him out of his bad mood, I heard from across the kitchen, *"Lorelai, stop it."*

Those three words stopped me in my tracks. My brother's words shocked me back into the reality that I didn't want to follow this pattern anymore. I wanted to change.

And I did. Realizing what I was doing, I lowered my voice and stopped acting like the peppy spokesperson for Christmas dinner. I went back to my cooking and stuck with the plan I created. I stopped allowing myself to be controlled by my Dad's mood and displeasure and let go of the tension and pressure to make everyone happy.

Mentally, I went to war with the tendency inside of myself and determined this pattern would not continue. The next time the lack of ham came up, I suggested my Dad go to the store, buy a ham, and put it in the oven. I never heard about it again.

You may be reading this and thinking, *"I can skip this chapter because it doesn't apply to me. I do not need to be cute or please people, be funny or do whatever it takes to make people nice to me. Not my problem."*

However, I encourage you to keep reading because this chapter isn't about HOW you react; it's about winning the battle over your natural reactions and bringing your natural responses under the Lordship of Christ.

Here's the thing: as we grow up, we are all affected by the people and situations around us. We all develop patterns for dealing with tension, difficult people, mistreatment, and maybe even abuse. I tend to cower and become agreeable and cute, but others do the opposite.

Other people are super angry and cruel to keep people in line. When they are hurting, they fight back. When they sense tension or even the possibility that they will be mistreated, they take the first shot to protect themselves, saying the nastiest things.

Some people hide and avoid conflict at all costs.

Other people use manipulation or even sexuality to diffuse a situation. Some even develop addictions to alcohol, drugs, food, or even hurting themselves to deal with the pain.

Whatever the method, these are all behaviors that we have learned to diffuse painful situations, stop abuse, or win a battle.

While others may look from the outside and say, *"Why do they act that way?"* the Heavenly Father Who knows all and sees all, recognizes that these behaviors are just cries from a little child or young person who wants the pain to stop and uses whatever tools are at their disposal to make it happen.

Mind-Blowing Truths
There's not much we can do to change the people or circumstances in our lives. However, as we cooperate with the Holy Spirit, He can change how we respond.

But here's the good news: even though the Heavenly Father understands why we do what we do, He doesn't leave us in our broken state. Instead, His perfect will is to show us that all these weapons we rely on are just worldly, unreliable means of fighting our battles that often cause us more pain than victory.

This is not how God wants His children to fight. Instead, He wants us to see our battles through spiritual eyes and use our spiritual weapons to win our battles.

Taking Your Thoughts Captive

Here's another mind-blowing truth I've learned: There's not much we can do to change the people or circumstances in our lives. As Jesus said, **"In this world you will have trouble." (John 16:33, NIV)**

That's a fact. However, it's not the whole story.

We see this when we look at the verse in its entirety

> *I have told you these things, so that in me you may have peace. In this world you will have trouble. But take heart! I have overcome the world. (NIV)*

When we allow God to heal the issues in our hearts and minds, the Holy Spirit can teach us to fight our battles using our spiritual weapons rather than the weak, harmful, inadequate techniques we've used throughout our lives.

Okay, Adessa, isn't this what we've been talking about in this study—we need to allow the Holy Spirit to heal our hearts and get to the root of the strongholds in our lives to overcome them?

Absolutely!

But there's one last thing we need to discuss:

Mind-Blowing Truths
When we allow God to heal the issues in our hearts and minds, the Holy Spirit can teach us to fight our battles using our spiritual weapons rather than the weak, harmful, inadequate techniques we've used throughout our lives.

Even after you've done the work, recognized that there is a stronghold in your life, identified the root, and done the work so your heart can be healed and the stronghold removed, there will still be challenging people and circumstances in your life.

Even though you've fought the fight and won the battle in your mind, when challenges arise, a part of you will want to revert to your old way of thinking and responding.

Why?

"Because that's what you always did." It's like muscle memory.

It's what happened to me a few days before Christmas. Remember: I'd already identified the problem.

The Holy Spirit used a television show to point out an area that needed to change. I agreed with Him and worked to get to the root of the stronghold and tear it down. I even asked my brother to hold me accountable.

Yet, when I was in a tense situation, my unconscious muscle memory wanted to return to my old behaviors.

Why was this happening? Hadn't I really gained victory?

Here's the thing: even after we gain victory in an area and take back ground from our enemy, that doesn't mean that he will go away in defeat. Instead, he will wait until just the right time—when your defenses are down or when you're in a difficult situation to try to gain a foothold again.

These are the times when you must recognize what's happening and say, *"Nope. Not happening. I already fought that battle and won—I'm not going back."*

Then, you use the spiritual weapons God has given you to fight the skirmish and hold your ground.

How do you do this?

1. As it says in 2 Corinthians 10:5, we need to take our thoughts captive.

Here's an example of what this means:

Recently, I was texting with a friend who was taking some classes. She had previously shared with me that she knew these classes were the next step in fulfilling God's plan for her life. When I asked her how her classes were going, I was surprised to hear that she'd stopped taking them. When I asked, *"Why?"* She said she was afraid. Whenever she took a class, someone in her family had a health issue.

I immediately felt the Holy Spirit lead me to say, *"That's superstition. I understand because I've sometimes fallen into that thought pattern, but the two things are not related. Superstition has no power over a child of God. These thoughts are lies from the enemy trying to keep you from doing what you know you should do."* We continued talking. I shared some Scriptures and told her to call me the next time she was afraid, and we'd pray together.

Sounds pretty spiritual, right?? Good job, Reverend Adessa!

But here's the funny thing: a few days later, I was walking down the same path of fear. As I prepared to do something, all I could think was, *"The last time we did this, something bad happened—maybe we shouldn't do it again."*

Immediately, I remembered my words to my friend: that's superstition—God doesn't want His children living in fear.

Now it was my turn to choose to *"take my thought captive"* and say, *"Hey, you crazy thought. Get out of my head. You are a liar. You can't stay here."*

Then, I followed Jesus' example when He was tempted and used God's Word to show these thoughts the way out the door.

> *For God has not given us a spirit of fear; but of power and of love and of a sound mind. -2 Timothy 1:7 (NKJV)*

> *The Lord directs the steps of the godly. He delights in every detail of their lives. -Psalm 37:23 (NLT)*

That's what it means to *"take your thoughts captive."* You recognize the thoughts that follow old patterns, realize they are wrong, and choose to think another way.

> **Mind-Blowing Truths**
> Taking your thoughts captive means you recognize the thoughts that follow old patterns, realize they are wrong, and choose to think another way.

It's the same thing I had to do at Christmas when my brother's words jolted me into reality. I recognized my old thought patterns and said, *"Nope. Not going this way anymore."* Then, I continued fighting by following our next step.

2. Use your spiritual weapons to fight and win the battle.

What are our spiritual weapons?

They are laid out in Ephesians 6:13-17:

> *Therefore, put on every piece of God's armor so you will be able to resist the enemy in the time of evil.*
>
> *Then after the battle you will still be standing firm.*
>
> *Stand your ground, putting on the belt of truth and the body armor of God's righteousness.*
>
> *For shoes, put on the peace that comes from the Good News so that you will be fully prepared.*
>
> *In addition to all of these, hold up the shield of faith to stop the fiery arrows of the devil.*
>
> *Put on salvation as your helmet, and take the sword of the Spirit, which is the word of God. (NLT)*

When I was a young girl, I was taught that *"putting on the whole armor of God"* meant that as you got dressed every morning, you read through these verses and put on your *"spiritual armor"* while you put on your clothes. While this wasn't harmful in any way, I'm not sure it was actually helpful either because choosing to wear the armor of God isn't a matter of ritual.

It's choosing to lay down the techniques, behaviors, and weapons we formerly used to protect ourselves and choosing to face each situation using the spiritual weapons God gives us.

- **Truth:** We can speak truth to ourselves and throw down the enemy's lies.

- **God's righteousness:** We can choose to put on righteousness and live righteous lives by following God's Word through the power of the Holy Spirit.

- **Peace:** Jesus said we would have trouble in this world, but He didn't end there. He also promised to give us His peace. We can choose to walk in His peace even during the most challenging situations.

- **Faith:** We can choose faith over fear in our lives and truly believe that God works all things together for the good of those who follow Him.

- **Salvation:** We can choose to have an eternal perspective, realizing the promises that come from our salvation.

- **The Word of God:** We can base our lives on God's Word—believe it, trust it, and live each day according to its principles.

Let's return to my story of the Christmas ham as an example of how these weapons can be practically used in our lives.

As I said, the first step was taking my thoughts captive, recognizing I was returning to old behavioral patterns, and deciding, *"Nope, not doing this anymore."*

The next step was fighting my mental battles using spiritual weapons like:

- **Truth:** I do not deserve to be mistreated or abused. I do not have to take it; I can remove myself from the situation or ignore it. It's not my job to make the whole world happy, take care of everyone, and make sure everyone's life is perfect. I make the best decisions I can and move on.

- **Faith:** I do not have to fear the future—I can trust God.

- **Peace:** I do not have to live in tension; I can choose to walk in peace. I can laugh, have fun, and enjoy my life even if someone else is unhappy.

- **Righteousness:** I can *"put on"* righteousness even if someone else does not. I can choose to behave and respond in a godly manner and be kind without being childlike.

- **Salvation:** I am a daughter of the most High God. My identity is found in Him, not in what I do. I can rest in the truth that God loves me no matter what.

- **Word of God**: I will fill my mind with the truth of God's Word and see life from His perspective.

> **Mind-Blowing Truths**
>
> You get stronger every time you take your thoughts captive and use God's weapons to win a skirmish. Victory comes as every day you choose to fight for your freedom.

You see, it's all so practical! Day by day, we continue to fight and win the skirmishes in our minds using the weapons of truth, faith, peace, righteousness, salvation, and the Word of God.

Here's an incredible truth: You get stronger every time you take your thoughts captive and use God's weapons to win a skirmish.

Taking Your Thoughts Captive

Victory comes as every day you choose to fight for your freedom.

Every battle you win strengthens you until the enemy finally realizes, *"I can't win this battle. They aren't returning to their old ways. I should just move on."*

But the choices lies with each of us.

Do we want to change?

Do we want victory and change enough to fight for it?

Are we open to the Holy Spirit showing us the truth?

Are we willing to do the work necessary to experience true healing and learn new ways of living?

Will we risk laying down the ways we've learned to fight our battles and learn to do things in God's way?

When the Holy Spirit calls your name and says, *"It's time to change,"* how will you respond?

Unfortunately, you can return to your old thoughts and behavioral patterns. Or you can do what it says in Ephesians 6:13 and stand firm.

> ***Therefore, put on every piece of God's armor so you will be able to resist the enemy in the time of evil. Then after the battle you will still be standing firm. (NLT)***

Each day, I choose to stand firm and fight.

Even though it's been challenging and painful, and it's taken me down roads I never expected to travel, I can genuinely say it's been worth every step.

The results have been life-changing and mind-blowing. I want the same for you.

So be strong and courageous, and choose to use the weapons God has given us to win the battles in your life.

Group Study Questions ...

1. List some ways people respond to stress, trauma, or challenging situations.

2. How can we overcome our natural tendency toward unhealthy responses and behaviors?

3. What does it mean to take our thoughts captive?

4. Read Ephesians 6:13-17. What are the spiritual weapons God has given us?

5. What does it mean to put on truth?

6. How do we put on righteousness?

7. How can we practically walk in peace?

8. How can faith act like a shield against the enemy's attacks?

9. The chapter defines wearing the helmet of salvation as "*choosing to have an eternal perspective, realizing the promises that come from our salvation.*" How do we do this?

10. How can we use God's Word to fight spiritual battles?

MIND-BLOWING TRUTHS: DEMOLISHING THE STRONGHOLDS IN YOUR MIND

Questions to Answer Privately ...

1. How do you usually respond in stressful or challenging situations?

2. Would you like to change this response?

3. This chapter was designed to give us a practical pattern to follow as we fight and win the battles in our minds. Thinking about the most recent mental battle you've faced, ask yourself these questions:
-How can I take my thoughts captive?

-How can I find the truth in this situation?

-How can I choose to put on righteousness in my responses?

-How can I walk in peace?

-How can I use faith as a shield against the enemy's lies?

-How does knowing who I am as a redeemed child of God and seeing things through an eternal perspective change my view of the situation?

-How can I use God's Word to battle the enemy's attack on my heart and mind?

4. What have you learned in this chapter, and how can it be applied to your life?

Take a moment and reread these key sentences, then journal what they mean to you. ...

1. As we grow up, we are all affected by the people and situations around us. We all develop patterns for dealing with tension, difficult people, mistreatment, and maybe even abuse. Whatever the method, these are all behaviors we learned to diffuse painful situations, stop abuse, or win a battle.

2. God wants us to see our battles through spiritual eyes and use our spiritual weapons to win our battles.

3. When we allow God to heal the issues in our hearts and minds, the Holy Spirit can teach us to fight our battles using our spiritual weapons rather than the weak, harmful, inadequate techniques we've used throughout our lives.

4. You get stronger every time you take your thoughts captive and use God's weapons to win a skirmish.

A Note From The Author

I hope you have enjoyed this book and, more importantly, that it has helped you experience freedom and gain victory in your life. Writing this book was a very personal experience for me, as I am not just passing along information; I lived through the process of tearing down strongholds. Every chapter is a lesson I learned and applied in my own life.

Along the way, there were plenty of tears, a little anger, and too many days when I wanted just to give up and say, *"This is ridiculous; I don't even care if I overcome these areas. It's too hard."*

During this time, the Holy Spirit reminded me of a quote from *Braveheart* that inspired me to keep fighting until I won the battle.

Let me set the scene.

Imagine an army of ragtag fighters standing in a line, carrying their makeshift weapons, ready to fight for their beloved Scotland, but more importantly, for their freedom.

That is, until they see the enemy.

Walking boldly in formation, clad in body armor, carrying swords and spears, the sight of the enemy makes them quake in their shoes. Completely intimidated and afraid, the amateur army begins to retreat.

That's when William Wallace appears on the scene and makes his famous speech, including these lines:

"You have come to fight as free men, and free men you are. What would you do without freedom? Will you fight?"

Then, a veteran soldier says: *"Fight? Against that? No, we will run, and we will live."*

To which Wallace replies: *"Aye, fight, and you may die. Run, and you'll live -- at least a while. And dying in your beds many years from now, would you be willing to trade all the days from this day to that for one chance, just one chance to come back here and tell our enemies that they may take our lives, but they'll never take our freedom!!!"*[1]

I've never been a huge fan of *Braveheart*. Still, the Holy Spirit used this quote to encourage me to keep moving forward and fighting for my spiritual freedom when I wanted to quit.

I was tired of drudging up painful memories, reliving fears, or facing the truth about people I loved. I have no desire to go through the heartache and agony.

I didn't have time to go to a counselor and do the homework they assigned. I definitely didn't want to spend the money.

Realizing the changes I needed to make seemed exhausting, overwhelming, and just too hard.

I was exhausted from fighting that battle.

I was also afraid to fight it. What if I went down the rabbit hole and couldn't deal with the truth I found? Even more petrifying was

A Note From The Author

the question of who I would be when the work of overcoming my past was over.

Like the men who wanted to run away in *Braveheart*, I wanted to take the easy way out, ignore my past and problems, and move on with life.

Then, the Holy Spirit brought this quote to my memory. It was like He was speaking the very words to me and saying, *"Yes, it will be easier to avoid the fight, but will you regret it later?"*

Because here's the thing: tearing down strongholds, finding healing, and becoming a sanctified follower of Jesus is not easy. It's literally a battle.

We can choose not to fight. We can choose to continue being oppressed by influences from our old ways of life, trapped in sin, heartache, and pain.

Many have chosen to walk away from the fight and live with the strongholds in their lives. They never remember things they didn't want to or face hard truths. They never see inside a counselor's office or spend hours journaling about their feelings.

But I wonder if those who make that choice someday don't look back on their lives and say, *"What could have been if I'd let the Holy Spirit do everything He wanted to do in my life? What if I'd been brave enough to let Him blow my mind, tear down every stronghold, remove every sin, and make me into everything He wanted me to be?"*

That *"what if"* made me decide I wouldn't take that chance.

The fact is that I don't want to wake up five, ten, or twenty years down the road and think, *"What could God have done with my life if I'd been courageous enough to fight the battle in my mind and overcome? Who would I be? How would my relationships be different? What would have happened if I'd been strong enough to fight?"*

Looking at it from this perspective, I made the same choice as the men in *Braveheart*.

I chose to fight. I decided to do the work. I determined that I would do whatever it took to overcome my past, gain healing and deliverance, and live the rest of my life in freedom.

Was it easy? No

Do I regret it? Not for a minute.

Because as William Wallace said, **"What is more valuable than freedom?"**[1]

Perhaps today, you are standing in your own line of decision. The Holy Spirit calls you to face your past or even the sins of your present and fight a spiritual battle to gain your freedom.

The choice is yours. Will you remain captive to the sins that so easily control you and the pain of your past, or will you rise like William Wallace and say, *"I want to be free?"*

Will you have your Braveheart moment, wear your spiritual armor, and cry, *"Freedom!"*

As someone who has been through this process, I wholeheartedly encourage you to go for it.

Allow the Holy Spirit to blow your mind, remove all the strongholds and lies, and do everything necessary to fight for your freedom.

Be brave. Be strong. And always remember, freedom is worth the process.

Thank you for taking this journey with me.

-Adessa

SCAN HERE FOR FREE VIDEO TEACHING FOR EACH CHAPTER

adessaholden.com/demolishingstrongholds

Bibliography

Chapter 1

1. Meyer, Joyce. *Battlefield of the Mind.* FaithWords, 1995. p. 8.

2. Frangipane, Francis. *The Three Battlegrounds.* Arrow Publications, 1989. p. 21.

3. Donald C, Stamps, *Article: Power Over Satan and Demons, Fire Bible:* English Standard Version, (Peabody, MA: Henderickson Publishers Marketing, LLC, 2014), Pg 1608.

4. Horton, Stanley M. *Systematic Theology: A Pentecostal Perspective.* Springfield, Mo: Logion Press, 1994. Print. Pg 399.

Chapter 2

1. Frangipane, Francis. *The Three Battlegrounds.* Arrow Publications, 1989. p. 35-39.

Chapter 4

1. *"Bless You, Hawkeye."* M.A.S.H, created by Larry Galbart, season 9, episode 17, Twentieth Century Fox, 1981.

2. Weber, Laverne, and Heidi Gregory. *Victory's Journey: Leaders Manual. Victory's Journey*, 2010. pp. 65-67.

3. Weber, Laverne, and Heidi Gregory. *Victory's Journey: Leaders Manual. Victory's Journey,* 2010. pp. 67.

Chapter 5

1. Donald C Stamps, *Study Notes on Romans 8:14, Fire Bible: English Standard Version,* (Peabody, MA: Hendrickson Publishers Marketing, LLC, 2014), Pg 1903.

2. *Creed.* Directed by Ryan Coogler, performances by Michael B. Jordan and Sylvester Stallone , Metro-Goldwyn-Mayer Pictures New Line Cinema Chartoff-Winkler Productions, 2015.

Chapter 6

1. Meyer, Joyce. *Battlefield of the Mind.* FaithWords, 1995. p. 8.

Chapter 7

1. Holden, Adessa. *Finding Healing.* Published by 4One Ministries. 2017.

Note From The Author

1. *Braveheart.* Directed by Mel Gibson, performances by Mel Gibson and Sophie Marceau, Paramount Pictures (United States and Canada) 20th Century Fox (International), 1995.

In *Mind-blowing Truth: Steps to Healing*, you will discover steps and tools to partner with the Holy Spirit and find healing and victory in your life.

This practical study explains the steps to healing, how you can put them into practice, and even how you might feel or the struggles you may face along the way. Each chapter also has a workbook section with questions to answer, Scriptures to ponder and memorize, and a place to journal about what the Holy Spirit speaks to you.

This book offers you what you need most: hope and practical steps to healing.

Visit adessaholden.com for details.

Available in print and digital formats.

ABOUT THE AUTHOR:

Adessa Holden is an ordained minister with the Assemblies of God, an author, a speaker, and a Bible teacher. She is a passionate individual who dedicates her life to these roles, inspiring others with her commitment.

Adessa is also the Vice President/Treasurer of 4One Ministries. She and her brother travel to speak, hold Mantour conferences, and produce resources. Their work provides practical Biblical teaching that strengthens, encourages, and challenges individuals to grow in their walk with Christ and apply Biblical principles to their everyday lives.

She graduated from the University of Valley Forge in 1996 with a degree in pastoral ministry and has continued studying God's Word ever since.

She's excited to share her newest project, **"Mindblowing Truths,"** a series of topical Bible studies designed to help individuals and small groups learn the mind-blowing truths in God's Word and practically apply them in their lives.

She's also written several women's books, including **"Finding Healing."** She also co-wrote **"Whatever It Takes"** with her brother, Jamie.

If you ask her about herself, she will tell you, *"I'm a minister, an author, a sister, and a daughter. The most important thing in my life is my relationship with Jesus, which began when I was just five years old, and I hid behind the sofa in our house and asked Jesus into my heart. Two years later, I received my call into full-time ministry. Following Jesus and studying God's Word have been my passion throughout my life. It's my most incredible honor and privilege to share the testimony of the healing the Holy Spirit has done in my heart, the difficulties He's helped me overcome, and the truth I've learned from God's Word. My life's goal is to encourage others to develop a personal relationship with Jesus and experience God's freedom and healing for themselves. Using every means possible, I want to reach people for Jesus."*

www.ingramcontent.com/pod-product-compliance
Lightning Source LLC
Chambersburg PA
CBHW050909160426
43194CB00011B/2340